The Samurai Treasure
サムライ・トレジャー

Let's Read a Mystery and Master Grammar

推理小説を読んで文法を征服しよう！

宮田 学 ❖ 編著
Manabu Miyata

トーマス・バゥアリー ❖ 原作
Thomas Bauerle

萌文書林
houbunshorin

はじめに

　高校時代に「英文法」の授業と聞くと、とたんに学習意欲が低下したという経験はありませんか？　そんなあなたは、「英文法」に拒否反応を示す、わが国の高校生としては平均的な生徒だったと言えます。文法用語がたくさん出てくるし、英文の構造を細かく分析し、それに見合った厳密な日本語訳を求められることが多く、退屈でつまらない授業になりがちだったからでしょう。

　このテキストは、そんな「英文法」を少しでもおもしろく学習できるようにと企画されました。オリジナルの推理小説 *"**The Samurai Treasure**"* を読み進みながら、その小説に出てくる英文を素材にして「英文法」を再学習し、使える道具に仕立てようというものです。

　「英文法」は、英語という言語を理解するための道具です。日本人の「英文法」が実際の場面に役立つ道具になっていない理由の1つは、各文法項目がバラバラに学ばれたままで、有機的に結びついていないからです。例えば、英文を読んでいると頻繁に出てくる単語の1つにthatがありますね。指示代名詞、接続詞、関係代名詞などという項目のもとで、それぞれの文法事項を学ぶものの、thatという単語に着目して統一的に学ばないために、道具としての切れ味が悪いのです。

　そこで、このテキストでは、学習者にある程度の文法知識が備わっているという前提で、バラバラに学習した内容をまとめ直す際の鍵となることばや項目に絞って学習できるように工夫しました。thatであれば、それが英文中で果たす役割を「英文解釈」の立場から分類し直し、thatを通して英文の構造を見直すことができるようにしたのです。各ユニットのGrammar for Comprehensionでは、このような方針で、andの用法、〜ingの用法、接続詞の用法、仮定法などを扱います。

＊

　このようにしてでき上がったテキストは12のユニットで構成され、各ユニットが以下の5つのセクションに分かれています。

Vocabulary

　そのユニットの *"**The Samurai Treasure**"* に出てくる未習語や難しい語句の発音と意味を確認するセクションです。

Listening

　イラストを見ながら、そのユニットの"*The Samurai Treasure*"を音声で聞き、日本語の質問に答えるセクションです。

Reading

　"*The Samurai Treasure*"の物語を12に分割し、順に読み進むセクションです。全文和訳を避け、物語の概要を把握するための多肢選択の問題［Exercise A］、指定された箇所について詳しく読み取るための問題［Exercise B］に取り組みます。［Exercise B］では、文脈の把握、発言の趣旨や意図、場面のイメージ化などの問題のほか、そのユニットで取り上げた項目を含む英文や構造が複雑な英文についてのみ日本語訳を求めます。

Grammar for Comprehension

　英文解釈に必要な文法知識を整理するセクションです。高校までの文法学習を前提に、英文を正確に読み取るためのコツを伝授する解説と練習問題で構成します。まず、［Questions］の質問に答えてから、その解答と解説を［Check Your Answers］で読み、最後に［Exercise］の練習問題に取り組むことになります。［Questions］や［Exercise］で取り上げる英文は、すべて"*The Samurai Treasure*"に出てくるものです。

補足

　Grammar for Comprehensionの解説部分は必要最小限の内容に絞り込むので、その不足を補うための追加ならびに英文法の全体像をつかむためのセクションです。

＊

　このテキストの学習が終わるころには、一篇の推理小説を読み終えるとともに、英文解釈に必要な実践的文法力を身につけることができます。これを踏み台にして、英文で書かれた新聞・雑誌・小説などに挑戦してください。Good luck！

2014年11月

編著者

The Samurai Treasure
Contents

Unit 1 　**語と句** ·· 6

　　"The Samurai Treasure" Part 1

Unit 2 　**自動詞・他動詞・準動詞** ······································ 14

　　"The Samurai Treasure" Part 1 (continued)

Unit 3 　**句と節** ·· 22

　　"The Samurai Treasure" Part 1 (continued)

Unit 4 　**And の用法** ··· 30

　　"The Samurai Treasure" Part 2

　　Column 1　知らない単語が出てきたら　　38

Unit 5 　**仮定法** ·· 39

　　"The Samurai Treasure" Part 3 & Part 4

Unit 6 　**倒置・挿入・省略** ··· 48

　　"The Samurai Treasure" Part 5

Unit 7 5W1H ……………………………………………………………… 55

"The Samurai Treasure" Part 6 & Part 7

Column 2 耳に聞こえる英語の音　64

Unit 8 接続詞の用法 ……………………………………………………… 65

"The Samurai Treasure" Part 8 & Part 9

Unit 9 That の用法 ……………………………………………………… 74

"The Samurai Treasure" Part 10

Unit 10 照応語句 ………………………………………………………… 82

"The Samurai Treasure" Part 11

Unit 11 ～ing の用法 …………………………………………………… 89

"The Samurai Treasure" Part 12

Column 3 "No, thank you." と言ったら……　96

Unit 12 総復習 …………………………………………………………… 97

"The Samurai Treasure" Part 13

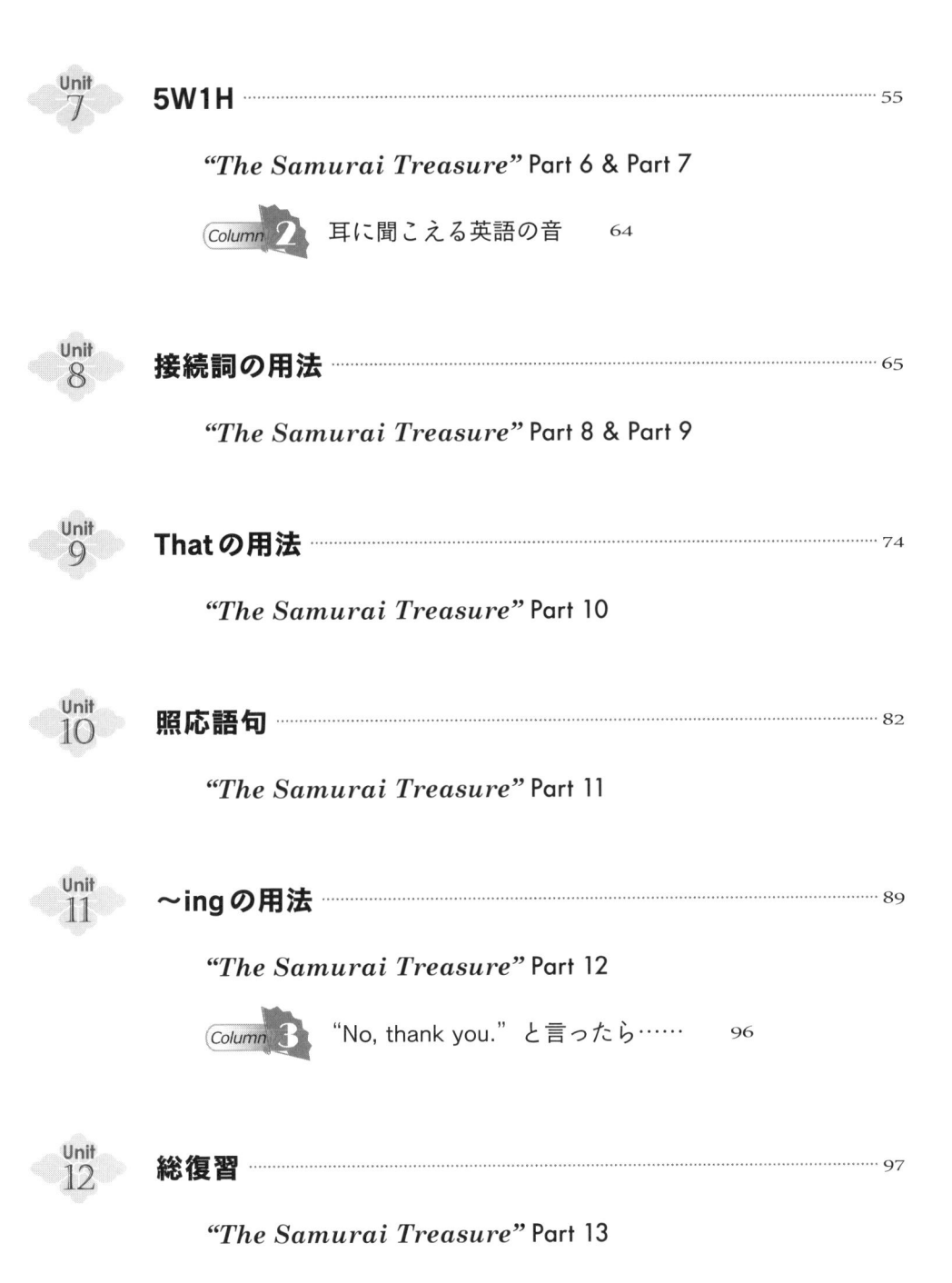

著者紹介　105

Unit 1

Let's Read a Mystery and Master Grammar

語と句

Vocabulary 次の語句の意味を確かめ、音声のあとについて発音しなさい。 　Track 1

clan [klǽn] 名C 一族
stand [stǽnd] 名C 抵抗、防御
tidal wave [táidl wéiv] 名C 津波
sword [sɔ́ːd] 名C 刀、剣
ancestor [ǽnsestə] 名C 先祖
hid [híd] ＜ hide [háid] 自動 隠れる
take over：引き継ぐ

Listening イラストを見ながら *"The Samurai Treasure"* の冒頭部分を音声で聞き、次の質問に答えなさい。 　Track 2

問1　Daisuke（大輔）少年は、どこで誰と話しているのでしょうか？
問2　二人はどんな話をしていますか？

Reading *"The Samurai Treasure"* の話を読み、下の設問に答えなさい。

Part 1   Daisuke and His Ancestor

"(1)This," said Father, "is the place where the Kinoshita clan made their last stand : a small group of samurai against many."

He and Daisuke stood on top of a small hill. Father pointed down the hill. "And the soldiers of the Maeda clan came up from below and ran over them like a tidal wave."

Daisuke looked down the hill through the trees and tried to imagine the samurai fighting with their swords in the forest. "And our great great great great grandfather...," he said.

Father smiled at Daisuke. "Our ancestor named Daisuke Kinoshita stood with the few samurai at the top of the hill. He fought bravely until his Daimyo was killed. Then he went with the few Kinoshitas who were still alive and hid in the forest."

"And I was named after Samurai Daisuke Kinoshita, right?" Daisuke said. (2)He knew the story but he loved to hear his father tell it.

"That's right," answered Father. "Samurai Daisuke hid in the forest until the war was over. Then he bought the forest, and our family still lives here to this day. Daisuke is a name that has been in our family for a long time. And you, young Daisuke, you will be a man soon. You are almost as tall as me already. Some day I may not be here, and you will have to take over. I have tried to teach a family lesson to you and your brother and sister : Be united and take good care of each other. I am sorry that we are a family that is '(3)land rich and money poor.' (4)We have nothing much but this piece of land with a lot of trees on it. And it is yours, too."

Exercise A — Choose the correct answer.

1. A boy named Daisuke
    a. is talking with his father at home.
    b. knows that his name was given by his grandfather.
    c. has an ancestor who fought for his master Maeda.
    d. wants his father to tell him about his ancestor.

2. Samurai Daisuke Kinoshita hid in the forest
    a. with his family members.
    b. with his Daimyo.
    c. until he was killed.
    d. until it was burned and destroyed.

3. Father expects
    a. that he will become rich and buy another piece of land.
    b. his children to be good enough to help one another.
    c. that a lot of trees will grow in their forest.
    d. his son to get taller and stronger than himself.

Exercise B — Answer the following questions.

問1 下線部(1)(2)(4)を日本語に訳しなさい。

問2 下線部(3)とはどういうことですか、日本語で説明しなさい。

問3 この話に登場するDaisuke（大輔）少年は何歳位だと思いますか、そう判断する理由とともに答えなさい。

Grammar for Comprehension (問題)

英文を正しく読み取るためには、文中における単語の役割を知ることが重要です。それぞれの単語が文中で果たす役割を分類したものを「品詞」と言います。英語の語（単語）と句について理解するために、まず、品詞について考えてみましょう。

Questions

Q1 英語の品詞はいくつあるでしょう？

Q2 次の各文中の同じ品詞の単語に下線を施しました。その品詞名がわかりますか？

1. He *and* Daisuke stood on top of a small hill.
2. He went with the few Kinoshitas who were still alive *and* hid in the forest.
3. Daisuke knew the story *but* he loved to hear his father tell it.
4. Then he bought the forest, *and* our family still lives here to this day.
5. We have nothing much but this piece of land with a lot of trees on it.

Q3 上の文でイタリック体になっている語（*and*と*but*）の品詞は何でしょうか？

Q4 「句」とは何でしょう？ 句にはどんなものがありますか？

Check Your Answers

クラスでQuestionsに対する答えを確認してから、Exerciseの練習問題に進みなさい。Questionsについての詳しい説明は、解説を参照しなさい。

Exercise 1 Q2の5つの文について、下線を施した単語の品詞を指摘しなさい。

1. He and Daisuke (1)stood on top of (2)a (3)small hill.
2. He (4)went with the few (5)Kinoshitas who (6)were still alive and (7)hid (8)in the (9)forest.
3. Daisuke knew the (10)story but he loved to hear (11)his (12)father tell (13)it.

4. Then he bought the forest, and (14)our family still (15)lives here to (16)this day.
5. (17)We have (18)nothing (19)much but this (20)piece of land with a lot of trees on it.

Exercise 2 次の文の下線を施した語群が形容詞句、副詞句のどちらであるかを指摘しなさい。

1. He and Daisuke stood (1)on top (2)of a small hill.
2. He went (3)with the few Kinoshitas who were still alive and hid (4)in the forest.
3. Then he bought the forest, and our family still lives here (5)to this day.

Exercise 3 次の文で下線を施した単語について、その品詞と意味を考えてから辞書を引き、調べた結果を答えなさい。

1. A small group of samurai against many.
2. The soldiers ran over them like a tidal wave.
3. Father led him to a nearby clearing in the forest.
4. He cupped his hands to his mouth and shouted.
5. It is the only piece of land that they don't own in the area.

Grammar for Comprehension（解説）

1 品詞とは？

　品詞というのは、文中における各単語の役割を整理・分類したものであり、英語の品詞は8つの役割に分類されます。次の図を参考にして、以下の解説を読んでください。

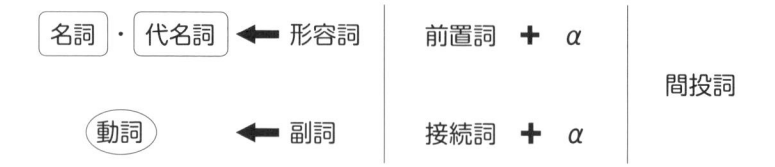

名詞・代名詞 ← 形容詞　　前置詞 ＋ α

　　　　　　　　　　　　　　　　　　　間投詞

動詞 ← 副詞　　　　　　接続詞 ＋ α

❷ 名詞・代名詞と形容詞の関係

　単語のレベルでみると、英文の中核（＝主語・目的語・補語・述語動詞）となるのは名詞・代名詞・動詞です。名詞と代名詞は、日本語でいう「体言」に相当すると考えてよいでしょう。この名詞・代名詞を修飾する（つまり、連体修飾語となる）のが形容詞です。

　Q2の1番で下線を施した単語はすべて名詞、文頭のHeは代名詞です。2番の単語はいずれも形容詞です。このうち、aliveは補語として用いられていますね。つまり、whoの先行詞であるKinoshitasがどんな状態であったのかを説明しています。形容詞には、名詞・代名詞を修飾する連体用法に加えて、この場合のように叙述用法もあります。また、theは名詞forestを修飾しているので形容詞です。冠詞のa/anとtheは形容詞の仲間なのです。

❸ 動詞と副詞の関係

　動詞は、日本語の「用言」の1つである動詞と同一に考えてよいでしょう。述部を構成する際になくてはならない不可欠なことばです。副詞はこの動詞を修飾する（連用修飾語の）役割を主に担っていますが、形容詞やほかの副詞を修飾することもあります。

　Q2の3番で下線を施した単語はすべて動詞です。ただし、knewとlovedは述語動詞ですが、hearとtellは不定詞となっています。4番の単語はすべて副詞ですね。Thenは彼が購入したのはいつだったかとboughtを修飾し、stillとhereはlivesを修飾して、いつどこに住んでいるのかを説明していることがわかります。

❹ 語レベルから句レベルへ

　語レベルで文の構成機能を果たすのは、以上のように、名詞・代名詞・形容詞・動詞・副詞という5つの品詞です。そして、英文の構造を考えるとき、

　　①名詞・代名詞　と　②それを修飾（説明）する形容詞
　　③動詞　　　　　と　④それを修飾（説明）する副詞

という図式が役立ちます。しかも、この図式は句のレベルにも適用できるのです。

「句」というのは、2語以上の単語がまとまって文中で1つの役割を担うときに、それらの語群を指して呼ぶことばです。英文解釈のためには、名詞句・形容詞句・副詞句の理解がポイントとなります。このうち、形容詞句と副詞句を形成する際に中心的な役割を担うのが前置詞なのです。前置詞はその名の通り、何かの前に置かれることばであり、必ず（と言ってよいほど）後ろに〈+α〉があります。この〈前置詞+α〉全体で形容詞や副詞の役割を果たすのです。

　Q2の5番で下線を施した単語はすべて前置詞です。このうち、of は land や trees をともなって of land, of trees という形容詞句を形成していますが、piece of ～、a lot of ～ という成句となっているため、その形容詞的役割を理解しづらいかもしれません。これに比べると、with a lot of ～ や on it が形容詞句となって land や trees を修飾していることはよくわかりますね。

　Q3の答えは接続詞です。厳密には等位接続詞と呼ばれるもので、語・語句・文を対等の位置に結びつける役割を果たします。1番の文の and は He と Daisuke という2つの名詞・代名詞を結び、2番の and は述語動詞 went と hid を結び、3番と4番の but や and は前後2つの文を結んでいます。

　では、5番の文中にある but も接続詞でしょうか？　接続詞であれば、but の前後に対等に結ばれるものがあるはずなのに、ありません。この but は、「～以外」という意味を表す前置詞としての役割を果たしているのです。❶で述べたように、「文中における単語の役割を整理・分類したもの」が品詞でした。1つの単語がいつも同じ役割を果たすとは限りません。それぞれの語が文中でどのような役割を果たしているのかを見きわめる必要があるのです。

補足1

　代名詞は、名詞の「代わり」という以上の重大な役割を担っています。例えば、中学1年生のころにおぼえた I, my, me; you, your, you などの「人称代名詞」は英文中になくてはならないことばなのです。

　英語の世界では、話し手（書き手）の自分（一人称：I）と聞き手（読み手）となる相手（二人称：you）が中心となり、それ以外はすべて三人称（he, she, it, they）という切り方をします。名詞の繰り返しを避けるために、これらの人称代名詞がさかんに用いられるのです［→Unit 10参照］。

補足2

　〈前置詞+α〉は名詞の役割を果たすことはないので、前置詞で始まる語句が文の

主語や目的語になることはありません。これは、英文の構造を見きわめる際の1つの重要な目安となりますね。

補足3

冠詞は形容詞の仲間であることがわかりました。このように、これまで品詞と思っていたものがじつはある品詞の下位分類だったということがあります。ここで整理しておくので、確認しておきましょう。

代名詞	人称代名詞、指示代名詞、関係代名詞、疑問詞（疑問代名詞）
形容詞	冠詞（定冠詞と不定冠詞）
動　詞	助動詞、不定詞、動名詞、現在分詞、過去分詞、［準動詞］
副　詞	関係副詞、疑問詞（疑問副詞）

補足4

前置詞や接続詞は数が限られています。代名詞もそれほど多くありませんが、名詞・形容詞・動詞・副詞はたくさんあります。なかでも、名詞にいたっては無限にあると言ってもよいくらいです。20世紀なかばに考案されたベーシック・イングリッシュ（BASIC English）は、英語学習者の負担を減らす目的で、学ぶべき単語の数を850語まで絞り込んだのですが、そのうち600語が名詞でした。このことからもわかるように、英文を理解する上で名詞はきわめて重要な役割を果たします。

補足5

このユニットで学んだことをまとめておきましょう。英語には8つの品詞があり、その内、名詞・代名詞・形容詞・動詞・副詞の5つが単独で英文の構成に寄与します。前置詞・接続詞の2つは単独では役に立たず、必ず〈＋α〉を必要とします。間投詞（または感嘆詞）は、これら7つの品詞とはかかわることなく、文中で独立して働くことばなので、英文構造を理解する上では無視してかまいません。

Unit 2

Let's Read a Mystery and Master Grammar

自動詞・他動詞・準動詞

Vocabulary 次の語句の意味を確かめ、音声のあとについて発音しなさい。 Track 3

- treasure [tréʒə] 名CU 宝物
- dug [dʌ́g] ＜ dig [díg] 他動 掘る
- prayer [préə] 名CU 祈り、祈りのことば
- bubbling [bʌ́bliŋ] ＜ bubble [bʌ́bl] 自動 〈液体が〉泡立つ、湧き上がる
- hot spring [hát spríŋ] 名C 温泉
- leave out ～：～を省く、落す
- guard [gáːd] 他動 〈攻撃・危害などから〉守る、保護する
- clearing [klíəriŋ] 名CU （森林の）木や草のない空き地
- cup [kʌ́p] 他動 〈手などを〉杯状にする
- underneath [ʌ̀ndəníːθ] 前 ～の下に、下側で
- pat [pǽt] 他動 〈手のひらで〉軽くたたく

Listening イラストを見ながら "**The Samurai Treasure**" の続きを音声で聞き、次の質問に答えなさい。 Track 4

問1 二人は宝物の話をしています。誰が誰に贈った宝物ですか？

問2 宝物の話をしてから、二人はどこに出かけましたか？

問3 何のために出かけたのですか？

Reading 物語 *"The Samurai Treasure"* の続きを読み、下の設問に答えなさい。

Part 1 Daisuke and His Ancestor (continued)

"What about the treasure?" asked Daisuke.

Father laughed, "Where did you hear about a treasure?"

"Everybody knows about it," said Daisuke. "They say that before the Daimyo of the Kinoshitas fell, (1)<u>he gave Samurai Daisuke his treasure and told him to hide it where the Maedas would never find it</u>. So Samurai Daisuke dug a deep hole in the forest, put the treasure at the bottom and covered it over. Then he prayed to the God of the forest, '(2)<u>Please keep it safe from the enemy!</u>' The God of the forest heard his prayer and (3)<u>he sent water bubbling up from the ground to cover the treasure and hide it forever</u>. That is how the hot spring came to exist."

Father laughed again. "You left out (4)<u>the best part</u>," he said. "They say that the ghost of Samurai Daisuke still guards the treasure and keeps it safe."

"Is it true?" asked Daisuke. "Is the story true?"

Father laughed, took his son by the arm, and led him to a nearby clearing in the forest. They walked to a small pool of hot water that was lying there. "Look down into the water," said father. "Do you see any treasure in there?"

"No," said Daisuke.

"It is just a lovely little hot spring," said Father. He cupped his hands to his mouth and shouted. "Hey! Samurai Daisuke! Are you here? Are you guarding the treasure?"

"You see? Nothing," he said. "(5)If the ghost story were true, something should happen underneath the water. Don't believe everything you hear. (6)Since your mother died, the only treasure I have is you, your brother and your sister. (7)That's better than any gold or jewels." He smiled at Daisuke, patting him on the shoulder.

Exercise A — Choose the correct answer.

1. Samurai Daisuke received his Daimyo's treasure
   a. after the Daimyo was killed.
   b. while the Daimyo was alive.
   c. but lost it while he was fighting.
   d. and buried it in the backyard of his house.

2. The hot spring
   a. is said to have been made by the God of the forest.
   b. appeared when Samurai Daisuke dug a deep hole.
   c. has long been dry since Samurai Daisuke died.
   d. seems to be as precious as gold or jewels.

3. Who believes in the ghost of Samurai Daisuke?
   a. Father.
   b. His son Daisuke.
   c. Father and his son Daisuke.
   d. No one.

Exercise B — Answer the following questions.

問1　下線部(1)(2)(3)(5)(6)を日本語に訳しなさい。

問2　下線部(4)the best partというのはどんな内容ですか、日本語で答えなさい。

問3　下線部(7)のThatは何を指していますか、日本語で説明しなさい。

Grammar for Comprehension (問題)

このユニットでは、動詞の働きに注目して、その種類や用法について学びます。まず、次の質問に答えましょう。

? Questions

Q 1 自動詞と他動詞の違いがわかりますか？

Q 2 各文の下線を施した述語動詞は自動詞・他動詞のどちらでしょう？

1. They walked to a small pool of hot water.
2. It is just a lovely little hot spring.
3. The God of the forest heard his prayer.
4. He gave Samurai Daisuke his treasure.
5. He sent water *bubbling* up from the ground *to cover* the treasure.

Q 3 5番の文でイタリック体になっている *bubbling* は動詞の何という形でしょうか？

Q 4 5番の文でイタリック体になっている *to cover* は「不定詞」ですね。この場合の用法は、名詞的用法、形容詞的用法、副詞的用法のどれでしょう？

✔ Check Your Answers

クラスで Questions に対する答えを確認してから、Exercise の練習問題に進みなさい。Questions についての詳しい説明は、解説を参照しなさい。

Exercise 1

次の文の下線を施した動詞が自動詞、他動詞のどちらであるかを指摘しなさい。

1. He heard his father tell the story.
2. I've never heard of anyone going on his land.
3. Samurai Daisuke hid in the forest.
4. He hid the treasure forever.
5. He knew the story.
6. Everybody knows about it.

7. Daisuke <u>looked</u> down the hill through the trees.
8. Samurai Daisuke <u>dug</u> a deep hole in the forest, <u>put</u> the treasure at the bottom and <u>covered</u> it over.
9. The ghost of Samurai Daisuke still <u>guards</u> the treasure and <u>keeps</u> it safe.
10. Father <u>laughed</u>, <u>took</u> his son by the arm, and <u>led</u> him to a nearby clearing in the forest.

Exercise 2 次の文の下線を施した語句が名詞句、形容詞句、副詞句のどれであるかを指摘しなさい。

1. The soldiers (1)<u>of the Maeda clan</u> came up (2)<u>from below</u> and ran over them (3)<u>like a tidal wave</u>.
2. Daisuke tried (4)<u>to imagine</u> the samurai (5)<u>fighting with their swords in the forest</u>.
3. Our ancestor (6)<u>named Daisuke Kinoshita</u> stood with the few samurai (7)<u>at the top of the hill</u>.
4. He loved (8)<u>to hear his father tell it</u>.
5. He smiled (9)<u>at Daisuke</u>, (10)<u>patting him on the shoulder</u>.

Grammar for Comprehension（解説）

1　自動詞

　英語の平叙文では、まず文の話題の主となる主語（subject = S）が現れ、次にその主語がどうであるのか、どうしたのか、という述部が続きますね。その述部の先頭に来るのが述語動詞（predicate verb = V）です。述部の構成の仕方は、その中の語順も含めて、ひとえに、この述語動詞（V）にかかっています。

　このVが「走る」「歩く」「泳ぐ」というような人間や動物の基本的動作、「〜にいる」「〜に住む」のような存在や状態を示す場合には、基本的に〈S + V〉で主な要素が出つくし、あとは修飾語句（いつ、どこで、どんなふうに、どれくらい、というように文の中身をふくらますもの）となります。また、Vが主語についての性格や状態について「どんな具合か」「どのような人物か」などというようなことを述べる動詞であれば、主語の性質についてその属性を決定する語が不可欠となり、S = Cという

形で補語（complement = C）をその後ろにしたがえることになります。これらの動詞を「自動詞」と呼んでいるのです。

Ｑ２の１番の述語動詞walkedに続く語句は〈前置詞＋α〉となっており、主語の「彼ら」が「どこまで」歩いたかを説明する修飾語句（＝副詞句）となっています。２番のisの後ろに続く語句の中心はspringであり、主語の「それ」が何であるのかを説明する補語となっています。つまり、It = springという関係を示す文となっていることがわかりますね。

2　他動詞

Ｖが主語が行う種々の行為を示し、かつ、その行為のおよぶ対象が前提となっている場合には、行為を受ける人・ものをＶのすぐ後ろにともなうことになります。writeであれば書かれるもの、loveであれば愛されるもの、giveであれば与えられる人ともの、という具合ですね。この行為を受ける人・ものを目的語（object = O）と呼び、Oを後ろにしたがえる動詞を「他動詞」と呼んでいるのです。

Ｑ２の３番の述語動詞heardに続くhis prayerはその目的語になっており、主語（森の神）が何を聞いたのかを説明しています。４番では、主語のHeがSamurai Daisukeにhis treasureを与えたと２つの目的語がgaveの後ろに続いています。５番のsentも他動詞で、すぐ後ろに目的語のwaterがありますね。

3　準動詞

Unit 1で形容詞句・副詞句について解説しましたが、名詞句には言及しなかったことに気づきましたか。名詞句を形成する代表は、じつは動詞なのです。動詞が名詞句になるとは、何とも不思議なことですが、動詞は姿形を変えて、英文中で名詞・形容詞・副詞に相当する働きをするのです（＝名詞的用法、形容詞的用法、副詞的用法）。この働きを担う不定詞・動名詞・現在分詞・過去分詞を総称して、準動詞と呼んでいます。このうち、不定詞と動名詞が名詞句の働きをするのです。

準動詞の最大の特徴は、動詞としての性質を残したままで、ほかの語句と結びついて作用するということにあります。Ｑ２の５番の文をもう一度見てみましょう。

He sent water <u>bubbling up from the ground</u> <u>to cover the treasure.</u>

この文の主語はHe、述語動詞はsentであり、その後ろのwaterが目的語となって

いましたね。それ以外はすべて修飾語です。現在分詞bubblingからgroundまでの語句はwaterを修飾する形容詞句であり、不定詞to cover以下は「何のために」送ったのかを説明する副詞句です。そのbubblingには、up, from the groundと「どんな具合に」「どこから」とbubblingを修飾する副詞・副詞句が続き、coverにはその目的語にあたるthe treasureが続いていますね。動詞としての性質を残しているというのは、こういうことを指しているのです。

補足1

　Unit 1で学習したように、1つの単語がいつも同じ働きをするとは限りません。したがって、1つの動詞がいつも自動詞、いつも他動詞となるわけでもないのです。例えば、次の文のVはＱ２の３番と同様にhearですが、その後ろに副詞句〈前置詞＋α〉(about the treasure) が続いており、自動詞となっていることがわかりますね。

　　Where did you hear about the treasure?

　このように、述語動詞の目的語に相当する語句（動作がおよぶ対象となることば）が文中（普通は動詞のすぐ後ろ）にあるかどうかを見きわめてはじめて、自動詞・他動詞の区別ができるのです。各ユニットのVocabularyでは、動詞について 自 ・ 他 と区別していますが、あくまでも一応の目安にすぎません。

補足2

　英語のあらゆる文を単純化してその基本構造を分類すると、以下の５つになります。これが、いわゆる英語の「５文型」です。補語や目的語をとるかとらないかは、ひとえにVの表す状態、動作にかかっています。

S + V	第一文型（このVは完全自動詞と呼ばれる）
S + V + C	第二文型（V＝不完全自動詞）
S + V + O	第三文型（V＝完全他動詞）
S + V + O + O	第四文型（V＝授与動詞）
S + V + O + C	第五文型（V＝不完全他動詞）

補足3

動詞はじつにさまざまな形に変化します。述語動詞となる場合は、現在・過去・未来という基本三時制、進行形・完了形・完了進行形、さらには受動態と計24種類の形がありえます。これを一覧すると以下のようになります。

準動詞のうち、現在分詞はbe動詞とともに用いて「進行形」を形成し、過去分詞はhave動詞とともに用いて「完了形」を、be動詞とともに用いて「受動態」を形成しますね。いずれも述語動詞の一部となり、主語の動作や状態についてその諸相を微妙な形で表すのに役立っているのです。

能動態		受動態
1. They dig a hole.	現在	13. A hole is dug.
2. They dug a hole.	過去	14. A hole was dug.
3. They will dig a hole	未来	15. A hole will be dug.
4. They are digging a hole.	現在進行形	16. A hole is being dug.
5. They were digging a hole.	過去進行形	17. A hole was being dug.
6. They will be digging a hole.	未来進行形	18. A hole will be being dug.
7. They have dug a hole.	現在完了形	19. A hole has been dug.
8. They had dug a hole.	過去完了形	20. A hole had been dug.
9. They will have dug a hole.	未来完了形	21. A hole will have been dug.
10. They have been digging a hole.	現在完了進行形	22. A hole has been being dug.
11. They had been digging a hole.	過去完了進行形	23. A hole had been being dug.
12. They will have been digging a hole.	未来完了進行形	24. A hole will have been being dug.

Unit 3

Let's Read a Mystery and Master Grammar

句と節

Vocabulary 次の語句の意味を確かめ、音声のあとについて発音しなさい。 Track 5

bully [búli] 名C いじめっ子、がき大将；形 いじめっ子の
grandson [grǽnsʌ̀n, grǽnd—] 名C 男の孫
pick on ～：～をいじめる、いびる
drive [dráiv] 他動〈人〉を～〔の状態〕にする、追いやる
own [óun] 他動 所有する
keep to oneself：人付き合いしない

Listening イラストを見ながら *"The Samurai Treasure"* の続きを音声で聞き、次の質問に答えなさい。 Track 6

問1 自宅への帰り道で、Daisuke（大輔）少年は誰の話をし始めましたか？

問2 家で飼っている犬の名前は何ですか？

問3 Old Man Yamada（山田老人）という人物は、どんな人なのでしょうか？

Reading 物語 *"The Samurai Treasure"* の続きを読み、下の設問に答えなさい。

Part 1 Daisuke and His Ancestor (continued)

"Father," Daisuke said as they walked home through the forest. "Why do they still hate us?"

"Who?" asked Father.

"The Maedas," said Daisuke. "The three old sisters who live in the big house in town and their bully grandson Takuma. They say bad things about us and make all kinds of trouble. Big Takuma picks on Hide, Miki and me almost every day. (1)Yesterday he was going to beat up Hide until Tetsu came running up to bite Big Takuma on the leg."

Father laughed. "Tetsu is a good dog," he said. "(2)I wish I had seen the look on that bully's face when he got bit."

"I don't know why they hate us," Father said. "Maybe it's because I let them think there really is a treasure here. (3)It drives them crazy." He laughed and winked at Daisuke. "Or maybe it's because this little forest is the only piece of land that they don't own in the area."

(4)"That and Old Man Yamada's over there," Daisuke pointed. "Why don't they pick on him?"

"Nobody picks on Old Man Yamada," said Father. "A lot of people are afraid of him because he keeps to himself and no one ever sees him."

Daisuke and Father walked off in the direction of home.

"Papa," said Daisuke. "I still miss Mama."

"Yeah," said Father. "Me, too."

Exercise A Choose the correct answer.

1. The Maedas are
   a. Daisuke's friend and his three sisters.
   b. Hide's classmate and his three aunts.
   c. Miki's boyfriend and his family.
   d. Takuma, his grandmother and her two sisters.

2. Old Man Yamada
   a. lives in a big house in town.
   b. owns a piece of land near the forest.
   c. is often made fun of by the Maedas.
   d. sometimes comes and talks to Daisuke's father.

3. How many people are there in Daisuke's family including him?
   a. Three.
   b. Four.
   c. Five.
   d. Six.

Exercise B Answer the following questions.

問1　下線部(1)(2)(3)を日本語に訳しなさい。

問2　下線部(4)と言って大輔が指差した (pointed) ものは何でしょうか、日本語で答えなさい。

Grammar for Comprehension (問題)

これまでの学習で、英文を語レベルで理解するだけでなく、句レベルでも理解できるようになったはずです。このユニットでは、さらに節レベルの理解ができるように学習します。まず、次の質問について考えましょう。

? Questions

Q1 句と節の違いがわかりますか？

Q2 主節と従属節の違いがわかりますか？

Q3 各文の下線を施した語群は、名詞節・形容詞節・副詞節のどれですか？

1. "Father," Daisuke said <u>as they walked home through the forest</u>.
2. I let them think <u>there really is a treasure here</u>.
3. They are the three sisters <u>who live in the big house in town</u>.
4. This little forest is the only piece of land <u>that they don't own in the area</u>.
5. I don't know <u>why they hate us</u>.

Q4 2番の文で、thinkとthereの間に省略されている単語は何でしょうか？

✔ Check Your Answers

クラスでQuestionsに対する答えを確認してから、Exerciseの練習問題に進みなさい。Questionsについての詳しい説明は、解説を参照しなさい。

Exercise　次の文の下線を施した語群が何句、何節であるのかを指摘しなさい。

1. This is the place (1)<u>where the Kinoshita clan made their last stand</u>.
2. Samurai Daisuke hid (2)<u>in the forest</u> (3)<u>until the war was over</u>.
3. Daisuke is a name (4)<u>that has been in our family</u> (5)<u>for a long time</u>.
4. I have tried (6)<u>to teach a family lesson</u> (7)<u>to you and your brother and sister</u>.
5. Then he prayed (8)<u>to the God</u> (9)<u>of the forest</u>, "Please keep it safe (10)<u>from the enemy</u>!"

6. They walked (11)<u>to a small pool</u> (12)<u>of hot water</u> (13)<u>that was lying there</u>.
7. I wish (14)<u>I had seen the look</u> (15)<u>on that bully's face</u> when he got bit.

Grammar for Comprehension（解説）

1　句と節

　句と節は、いずれも語レベルでなく、まとまりのある語群が全体として1つの役割を担っています。英文の構造を正しく理解するには、句レベルで名詞句・形容詞句・副詞句、節レベルで名詞節・形容詞節・副詞節を区別することが大切です。まず語群としてのまとまりをつかみ、次にその役割を見きわめることが必要となります。

2　節

　節は、句と違って、その語群の中に〈主語＋述語動詞〉が温存されています。2つ以上の文がand, but, orなどの等位接続詞で結ばれている場合、結ばれた個々の文を等位節と呼び、その節の働きが何であるか（つまり、名詞節か形容詞節かなど）は問題となりません。

　それに対して、when, as, thatなどの従属接続詞で文と文を結んだ場合、いずれか一方が主節となり、接続詞で導かれた語群は、その主節の一部を修飾したり、主節の要素の一部（主語、目的語、補語）となったりして、いわば従属的な役割を果たすので従属節または従節と呼ばれています［→Unit 8参照］。

　これは、関係代名詞や関係副詞で導かれた節が主節の名詞要素を修飾する場合にもあてはまります。また、疑問文を平叙文の語順にして文中に組み入れた「間接疑問文」も従属節（名詞節）となります。

3　名詞節・形容詞節・副詞節

　Q3の1番の下線部は、接続詞asで導かれた副詞節を形成し、主節"Father," Daisuke saidに対する従属節となっています。2番では、thinkの後ろに接続詞thatが省略されていますね。下線部は名詞節で、他動詞thinkの目的語となっています。

　3番と4番の文では、関係代名詞が用いられています。3番では主格のwho、4

番では目的格のthatがあり、それ以下の語群を導いて形容詞節となっているのです。目的格の関係代名詞は省略できるので、4番のthatを省いた表現も可能ですね。現代英語では（とくに口語では）、接続詞のthatや目的格の関係代名詞を省くことが多いのです。

5番の文のwhyで始まる語群は間接疑問文で、他動詞knowの目的語（名詞節）になっていることは容易に理解できるでしょう。

補足1

すでにUnit 1とUnit 2で学んだように、前置詞と準動詞が句の形成に重要な役割を果たすのでした。例えば、Unit 2のExercise 2で取り組んだ以下の文では、下線部(a)の不定詞 to imagine は、動詞triedの目的語となる名詞句を形成していました。下線部(b)のfightingは現在分詞で、with their swords および in the forest という〈前置詞 + α〉（= 副詞句）をともなって、すぐ前のsamuraiを修飾する形容詞句の役割を果たしていました。

Daisuke tried (a)to imagine the samurai (b)fighting with their swords in the forest.

また、次の下線部(d)の不定詞 to bite Big Takuma は、犬のテツが「なぜ」走ってきたのかを説明する副詞句、下線部(e)の on the leg は「どこに」嚙みついたのかを説明する副詞句でした。では、下線部(c)の running up はどうでしょうか。この running が現在分詞であることは確かなのですが、何句でしょう？

Tetsu came (c)running up (d)to bite Big Takuma (e)on the leg.

これについては2通りの解釈がありえます。補語のような役割を果たしていると考えて形容詞句とする見解と、「〜ながら」という意味を表すことから副詞句と見なす立場とに分かれるでしょう。

最初に文法があってあとから言語ができたのではなく、その逆です。文法はあくまでも言語の仕組みや構造を説明するための道具であり、残念ながら、あらゆる言語現象を完璧に説明しきれないのです。したがって、この場合のように、異なる解釈が起こりうるのです。文法理論にそうした限界があることもおぼえておきましょう。

補足 2

a. 名詞句

不定詞または動名詞で導かれた語群が名詞句の働きをします。名詞に相当する働きをするので、主語・補語・目的語になります。動名詞の場合は前置詞の後ろに置くこともできるので、その場合は〈前置詞＋動名詞＋〜〉全体で形容詞句・副詞句の働きをすることになります。

I have tried to teach a family lesson to you.	不定詞／目的語
The three children began walking in the direction of home.	動名詞／目的語
Thank you for giving me the treasure.	動名詞／前置詞の後ろ

b. 形容詞句

〈前置詞＋a〉および不定詞・現在分詞・過去分詞で導かれた語群が名詞（代名詞）を修飾する働きをします。現在分詞と過去分詞は単独で名詞を修飾することがあり、この場合は「分詞→名詞」の語順となります。それ以外は、いずれも名詞のすぐ後ろからその名詞を修飾します。

We have this piece of land with a lot of trees on it.	前置詞＋a
Come on, it's time to go home.	不定詞
He imagined the samurai fighting with their swords in the forest.	現在分詞
Our ancestor named Daisuke Kinoshita stood at the top of the hill.	過去分詞

c. 副詞句

〈前置詞＋a〉に加えて、不定詞、現在分詞で導かれた語群が動詞を修飾する働きをします（形容詞や副詞を修飾することもあります）。

Daisuke looked down the hill through the trees.	前置詞＋a
Tetsu came running up to bite Big Takuma on the leg.	不定詞
He smiled at Daisuke, patting him on the shoulder.	現在分詞

補足 3

A. 名詞節

that, if, whether などの従属接続詞で導かれた語群、what などの関係詞で導かれた語群が文中で主語・補語・目的語の役割をしたり、前置詞の後ろに置かれたり、あるいは、名詞の同格として用いられたりします。間接疑問文も名詞節となります。

They say <u>that the ghost still guards the treasure</u>.	接続詞／目的語
<u>What people say about the treasure</u> is not true.	関係詞／主語
The fact is <u>that it is just a lovely little hot spring</u>.	接続詞／補語
I don't know <u>why they hate us</u>.	間接疑問文／目的語

B. 形容詞節

　関係代名詞、関係副詞で導かれた節がすぐ前の名詞（＝先行詞）を修飾するので、形容詞相当語句となります。先行詞をともなわない場合には、名詞節になります。

Then he went with the few Kinoshitas <u>who were still alive</u>.	関係代名詞
This is the place <u>where the Kinoshita clan made their last stand</u>.	関係副詞
cf. That is <u>how the hot spring came to exist</u>.	関係副詞→名詞節

C. 副詞節

　when, if, as などの従属接続詞で導かれた語群が、時・条件・原因・理由など、さまざまな意味を示して、主節の動詞を修飾します。

He fought bravely <u>until his Daimyo was killed</u>.	接続詞（時）
<u>If the story is true</u>, there must be a treasure here.	接続詞（条件）
I am sorry <u>that we are a family that is 'land rich and money poor.'</u>	接続詞（原因）

Unit 4

Let's Read a Mystery and Master Grammar

Andの用法

Vocabulary 次の語句の意味を確かめ、音声のあとについて発音しなさい。 Track 7

wiggle [wígl] 他動〈身体（の一部）など〉をぴくぴく［くねくね］小刻みに動かす；自動 ぴくぴく［くねくね］小刻みに動く

toe [tóu] 名C 足の指

lizard [lízəd] 名C トカゲ

attempt [ətémpt] 名C 試み、企て、努力

croak [króuk] 自動〈カラス・カエルなどが〉ガーガー［カーカー］鳴く

cardboard box [ká:dbɔ:d báks] 名C 段ボールの箱

lid [líd] 名C（箱・なべなどの）ふた

cotton candy [kátn kǽndi] 名U 綿菓子

sulfur [sʌ́lfə] 名 硫黄

beetle [bí:tl] 名C カブト虫

stuff [stʌ́f] 名U〈漠然と〉物、こと

emerge [imə́:dʒ] 自動 現れる、出てくる

sibling [síbliŋ] 名C（男女の別なく）きょうだい

overhead [òuvəhéd] 副 頭上に、空中で

crow [króu] 名C カラス

furry [fə́:ri] 形 柔毛で覆われた、ふわふわした

splash [splǽʃ] 他動〈水・泥など〉を飛び散らす、はねかける

Listening イラストを見ながら *"The Samurai Treasure"* の続きを音声で聞き、次の質問に答えなさい。

Track 8

Unit 4

And の用法

問1　Hidenori（秀典）と Miki（美樹）は、どこにいるのでしょう？
問2　美樹が話している Koko（ココ）とは何でしょうか？
問3　美樹にはどんな趣味があるのでしょう？
問4　Daisuke（大輔）は何をしにやって来たのですか？
問5　犬の Tetsu（テツ）はどんな悪さをしましたか？
問6　家に帰ろうとしたときに大輔が立ち止まったのはなぜでしょう？

Reading 物語 *"The Samurai Treasure"* の続きを読み、下の設問に答えなさい。

Part 2　Hide and Miki

A few days later, Hide and Miki were playing in the forest.

"Where's Daisuke?" asked Miki. "He usually comes by now and tells us to get home for dinner."

Hidenori wiggled his toes in the hot water before he answered. "I don't know," he said.

"Hide," asked Miki, "do you think he'll like Koko?"

"Who's Koko?" asked Hide.

Miki held up a small gray lizard that was wiggling in an attempt (1)to escape from her hand. "This is Koko. I just caught him."

"And you named him already?"

"Sure," said Miki. "(2)It was easy. Just listen."

She held the lizard (3)close to Hide's ear. The lizard stopped wiggling and looked at Hide with its two yellow eyes. It croaked at him twice. "Ko-ko!" it said. "Ko-ko!"

"I see where you got the name," Hide laughed. He watched as his little sister gently put the lizard inside a small cardboard box and (4)closed the lid.

"I almost got a snake earlier," she said.

"(5)Leave the snakes alone," said Hide. "We don't want you to bring any more of them inside the house with the rest of (6)your mini zoo. And look at you. (7)You've gotten your clothes dirty again, chasing animals all over the place."

Hidenori looked up at the setting sun. It was big and glowing orange. (8)Around it were long pink clouds that looked like the cotton candy he had bought for his little sister Miki at the local festival last summer. A soft breeze blew through the trees and the sky was beginning to turn dark purple.

"(9)This is perfect," he said. "Our own private place in the woods, with our own private hot spring (10)coming straight up out of the rocks in the ground." He wiggled his toes once more in the pool of hot water and enjoyed the strong smell of sulfur.

"And our own private snakes and lizards," said Miki.

"Yes," laughed Hidenori. "And rabbits and beetles and all the other crazy stuff you catch here and bring home."

"Hide!" A boy's voice called out to them through the trees ahead. "Miki! Where are you?"

"It's Daisuke!" said Miki. "Should we hide from him?"

"No," said Hidenori. "He's going to be a little mad that we stayed here (11)this late anyway. We'd better answer him."

"We're over here!" Hide said. "At the hot spring!"

A tall thin boy emerged from the trees and stepped into the clearing. Daisuke stopped and smiled at his two younger siblings (12)playing in their secret place. It was a place where the three of them loved to spend time together: a small clearing in the middle of the forest their family owned. It was the beginning of autumn, and the tree leaves all danced in the evening breeze. Overhead a crow called out and was answered by (13)another farther away. (14)Near the edge of the clearing was a small pile of stones where a natural hot spring bubbled up from the ground and formed a small pool about the size of a bathtub. Hide was pulling his feet out of it and putting on his shoes as Daisuke approached them.

"Where's Tetsu?" asked Miki.

At that moment a big, brown furry dog ran out of the woods and jumped into the hot spring pool, (15)splashing water all over Hide.

"There he is!" laughed Miki.

"Bad dog!" shouted Hide but he couldn't help laughing as the water ran down his face. Tetsu barked happily and ran from one kid to the other, shaking the water from his fur onto them.

"Come on, it's time to go home," said Daisuke. "Papa has made dinner for us."

The three children gathered together and began walking in the direction of home. Tetsu ran ahead barking happily.

"I caught a lizard, a beetle and three worms," said Miki, holding out her cardboard box for Daisuke to see.

"Wait," Daisuke said. He stopped suddenly, bent down and picked up something off of the ground. "What is this? WHAT IS THIS?"

Exercise A   Choose the correct answer.

1. It is
    a. early morning in spring.
    b. late at night in winter.
    c. around noon in summer.
    d. early evening in fall.

2. Hide and Miki
    a. are playing in the forest until it is time to go home.
    b. are both catching small animals in the forest.
    c. got lost and found a good place to stay overnight.
    d. came to the hot spring to enjoy swimming there.

3. Koko

    a. is a lizard that was wiggling in the hot water.

    b. is the name given by Hide when he heard it croak.

    c. was caught and put into a box by Miki.

    d. was joined by a snake that had been caught earlier.

4. Hide

    a. had forgotten to buy a cotton candy for his sister.

    b. doesn't want his sister to bring more animals to their home.

    c. loves the hot spring, but doesn't like its smell.

    d. got angry and wept when Tetsu splashed water all over him.

5. Daisuke

    a. came to find Hide and Miki, but they hid from him.

    b. told Hide to bring Tetsu back to the hot spring.

    c. laughed when he saw Tetsu jump into the hot water.

    d. called to Hide and Mike so that they should return for dinner.

Exercise B Answer the following questions.

問1　下線部(1)(10)(12)(15)が何句であるかを指摘しなさい。

問2　下線部(2)It, (9)This, (13)anotherはそれぞれ何を指しているか、日本語で答えなさい。

問3　下線部(3)と(4)のcloseの品詞と意味を日本語で答えなさい。

問4　下線部(5)(7)(8)(14)を日本語に訳しなさい。

問5　下線部(6)で秀典がyour mini zooと言っている理由を日本語で説明しなさい。

問6　下線部(11)thisの品詞と意味を日本語で答えなさい。

Grammar for Comprehension（問題）

　Unit 1で、接続詞andとbutについて簡単に学習しました。このユニットでは、その役割についてさらに詳しく学習します。次の質問について考えてみましょう。

Questions

Q 1 and が when, if, as などの接続詞と異なっているのは、どのような点でしょうか？

Q 2 各文の下線を施した and は何を結んでいますか？

1. He stopped suddenly, bent down <u>and</u> picked up something off of the ground.
2. Hide was pulling his feet out of it <u>and</u> putting on his shoes as Daisuke approached them.
3. A soft breeze blew through the trees <u>and</u> the sky was beginning to turn dark purple.
4. It was big <u>and</u> glowing orange.
5. And rabbits <u>and</u> beetles <u>and</u> all the other crazy stuff you catch here <u>and</u> bring home.

Check Your Answers

クラスで Questions に対する答えを確認してから、Exercise の練習問題に進みなさい。Questions についての詳しい説明は、解説を参照しなさい。

Exercise

次の文中の <u>and</u> が何を結んでいるのかを指摘しなさい。

1. Then he bought the forest, <u>and</u> our family still lives here to this day.
2. Father laughed, took his son by the arm, <u>and</u> led him to a nearby clearing in the forest.
3. The only treasure I have is you, your brother <u>and</u> your sister.
4. He usually comes by now <u>and</u> tells us to get home for dinner.
5. He watched as his little sister gently put the lizard inside a small cardboard box <u>and</u> closed the lid.
6. It was the beginning of autumn, <u>and</u> the tree leaves all danced in the evening breeze.
7. Overhead a crow called out <u>and</u> was answered by another farther away.
8. I caught a lizard, a beetle <u>and</u> three worms.

Grammar for Comprehension（解説）

1　andの基本的役割

　　Unit 1の解説で扱ったandは「等位接続詞」の代表です。等位接続詞の最大の特徴は、「同じものを同じ位置関係に対等に結びつける」という点にありました。「同じもの」とは、単語と単語、句と句、節と節、文と文ということであり、名詞と名詞、動詞と動詞、形容詞と形容詞、不定詞と不定詞、等々ということでもあります。

　　when, if, as などの従属接続詞は、普通、従属節の先頭に置かれて、その従属節を主節に結びつける役目をしますが、andは何でも結ぶことができるし、同じものを「対等の関係」に結びつけるのです。また、andは同じものなら、いくつでも結べます。3つ以上のものを結ぶときは、最後の要素の直前にandを置くのが原則です。

2　andが結ぶもの

　　Q2の最初の文で、andはstopped, bent, pickedと3つの動詞を結んでいます。3つ目のpickedが最後の要素となるので、その前にandが登場しています。「同じものを同じ位置関係に対等に結びつける」という基本通りに、いずれも過去形の述語動詞であり、主語Heが行った動作を順番に描写していますね。

　　andが何と何を結んでいるのかを見きわめるためには、A and BのBを特定するとよいでしょう。1番の文ではandのすぐ後ろにpickedという過去形の動詞があったので、「同じもの」という基準でstoppedとbentが見つかりました。2番の文を見ると、andのすぐ後ろにputtingという準動詞がありますね。この準動詞Bと「同じもの」がないかと前に目をやると、pullingがあります。したがって、A and BのAはpullingであり、過去進行形を形成する現在分詞がandで結ばれていることが判明します。3番の文を観察してみると、AがA soft breeze blew through the trees、Bがthe sky was beginning to turn dark purpleであり、andがその前後にある2つの文を結んでいることがわかります。

　　では、4番目の文のandは何と何を結んでいるのでしょうか。A and BのBはglowingですが、それと同じ～ingがandの前に見あたりません。Aと考えられるのは、bigという形容詞です。Aが補語、Bが進行形の～ingですが、wasに続く語として「同じ位置関係」に結びつけられています。このように、「同じもの」という厳密な

基準から外れることもあるので要注意です。

　最後の文では、andが4回も登場します。4つ目のandがcatch (here)とbring (home)を結んでいることは明らかですが、ほかの3つはどうでしょう？　普通ならばAnd rabbits, beetles and all the other crazy stuff you catch here and bring home.と言うはずで、このandがrabbits, beetles, (all the other crazy) stuffの3つを結ぶ役目を果たします。元の文のようにandをもう1つ入れたのは物事を羅列する効果を出すためで、「～も～も」という気持ちを表しています。Readingの該当箇所を読んでわかったように、妹の美樹のことばを受けて、"And..."と兄の秀典が発言したのであり、妹が森で見つけた昆虫を「次から次へと」家に持ち込む様子を言い表そうとしたのです。

🌱 補足

　等位接続詞には、andのほかにbutやorがあります。andと同様に、同じものを同じ位置関係に対等に結びつけます。以下の文中のbutやorが何を結んでいるかを考えてみましょう。

1. He knew the story but he loved to hear his father tell it.
2. That's better than any gold or jewels.
3. "Bad dog!" shouted Hide but he couldn't help laughing.
4. She didn't wait for an answer, but ran to her room.
5. It's probably just a squirrel or a rabbit.
6. I'll tell him, but I know his answer.
7. Thanks but she's not allowed to have candy before dinner.
8. There is a little money here, but not much.
9. I don't know, but it can't be good.
10. I keep to myself, but I watch what is happening in this town.

　1番、3番、6番、9番、10番ではbutの前後にある2つの文、2番と5番ではorの前後にある2つの名詞（goldとjewels、squirrelとrabbit）、4番ではdidn't wait (for an answer)とran (to her room)という2つの述語動詞をbutが結んでいます。

　7番は、ややわかりづらいかもしれませんが、butの前後にある2つの文を結んでいます。butの前にあるThanksは1語で文になっており、「ありがとう。でも～」と後ろの文に続いていることがわかります。また、8番はmuchの後ろにmoneyを補って考えるとよいでしょう。すると、There isの後ろに続く位置に、a little moneyとnot much (money)がbutで結ばれていることがわかりますね。

Column 1

知らない単語が出てきたら

　あなたは、自分が知らない単語（＝未知語）が出てくるとすぐに辞書で調べる、というクセがついていませんか？　大学受験や定期試験のときには辞書を引くことはできませんから、単語をたくさん知っていればいるほど、有利であることは確かです。しかし、これだけ覚えれば絶対大丈夫という上限はありません。そこで、未知語が出てきたら、その意味を文脈から判断する力が必要となってきます。

　例えば、exuberantという単語を知っているでしょうか？　単語だけではどんな意味かわからなくても、この単語が使われている次のような英文を読めば、その意味が推測できるはずです。

> *Jane* : How's Michelle doing? The last time I met her, she looked a little depressed and said she was worried about her schoolwork.
> *Mary* : I saw her yesterday, and she seemed absolutely exuberant.
> *Jane* : Really? I wonder what happened.
> *Mary* : Well, she'd been worried about her math test, but she did really well after all. Also, she's found a part-time job that she enjoys a lot.
> *Jane* : That's great. I'm happy to hear that.

　これは、2014年度のセンター入試で出題された問題です。受験生は与えられた4つの選択肢（busy and stressed, happy and energetic, hard-working and healthy, upset and nervous）から1つ選ぶのですが、正解はhappy and energeticですね。2人の会話から、Michelleはdepressed, worriedという状態だったのが、逆の状態になってよかったという文脈を読み取ることによって、正しい意味が推測できるのです。

　ひるがえって、自分がどれだけの日本語を知っているかを考えてみましょう。母語といえども、すべてのことばを知り尽くしているわけではありません。手元にある日本語の辞書の適当なページを開いてみてください。そのページに掲載されているすべてのことば（の意味）を知っていましたか？　きっと、知らないことばがあったはずです。日本語を聞いたり読んだりしているとき、未知語が出てきても、自分なりに意味を推測して理解しているのです。

　外国語である英語でも同じことです。一定程度の語彙力がついたら、未知語が出てきてもすぐに辞書で調べるのではなく、文脈から自分なりに意味を推測し、それから辞書を引いてその判断が正しかったかどうかを確かめるようにしましょう。英文で書かれた物語・新聞・論文などを読むときにはそうした力がきっと役立つことでしょう。

Unit 5

Let's Read a Mystery and Master Grammar

仮定法

Vocabulary 次の語句の意味を確かめ、音声のあとについて発音しなさい。 Track 9

butt ［bʌ́t］ 名 (タバコの) 吸いさし、吸い殻
disgust ［disgʌ́st］ 名U〈…に対する〉(むかつくような) 嫌悪
sniff ［sníf］ 自動〈人・物のにおいを〉くんくんかぐ
kind of ~：なんとなく、ちょっと~のよう
creepy ［kríːpi］ 形 身の毛がよだつ、ぞくぞくする
squeeze ［skwíːz］ 他動 強く握る
property ［prápəti］ 名U 財産、地所
squirrel ［skwə́ːrəl］ 名C リス
leash ［líːʃ］ 名C (動物をつなぐ) 綱、鎖
tattered ［tǽtəd］ 形 ぼろぼろに裂けた
wrinkled ［ríŋkld］ 形 しわの寄った
burst ［bə́ːst］ 自動 急に飛び出す、突進する
skinny ［skíni］ 形 やせこけた、骨と皮ばかりの
tadpole ［tǽdpòul］ 名C オタマジャクシ
cocoon ［kəkúːn］ 名C (チョウ・ガの幼虫) 繭 (まゆ)
dirt ［də́ːt］ 名U 土、ほこり
chunk ［tʃʌ́ŋk］ 名C (パン・肉などの) 大きな塊
ground ［gráund］ ＜ grind ［gráind］ 他動 すりつぶす、〈肉〉をひく
fridge ［frídʒ］ 名C 冷蔵庫［refrigeratorの短縮語］
disgusting ［disgʌ́stiŋ］ 形 気分の悪くなる

Listening イラストを見ながら *"The Samurai Treasure"* の続きを音声で聞き、次の質問に答えなさい。

問1　三人が足元に見つけたものは何でしょうか？
問2　見つけたものからどんなことを想像しましたか？
問3　三人が立ち去った後、どんな人物が現われましたか？

問4　美樹は台所に来る前にどんなことをしましたか？
問5　テーブルの上に何が置いてありましたか？

問6　美樹は冷蔵庫から何を取り出そうとしているのでしょうか？

問7　秀典は冷蔵庫の中に何を見つけましたか？

Reading 物語 *"The Samurai Treasure"* の続きを読み、下の設問に答えなさい。

Part 3　Cigarette Butts

The three stood looking at the ground in front of them. Two cigarette butts lay there in the grass. Daisuke threw down the one he had in his hand with disgust. That made three all together. Tetsu lowered his head and sniffed at the spot (1)where the cigarettes lay.

Daisuke said, "Who put these here? No one comes here except us."

"It looks like someone was standing behind this tree watching us," said Miki. "That's kind of creepy." She grabbed Hide's hand and held it (2)tight.

"No, it was probably just a man who got lost and was walking through the woods on his way home. Nothing to worry about," said Daisuke.

Tetsu raised his head, looked off into a far group of trees and began barking.

"Oh, Hide!" said Miki, squeezing his hand tighter. "Someone is there! Someone is watching us now!"

"That's in the direction of Old Man Yamada's property," said Hide. "They say if he catches any kids on his land, they disappear and are never seen again."

"No," said Daisuke. He grabbed Tetsu by the collar before he could run toward the trees. "It's probably just a squirrel or a rabbit. Don't be frightened by (3)those old stories." He reached into his pocket, took out a leather leash (4)and attached it to the dog's collar. "Let's go home. Supper is waiting."

He pulled Tetsu along by the leash as the three (5)headed for home.

As the children walked away from the clearing, a tall man stepped out of the trees and walked over to (6)where the cigarettes lay. He was wearing an old gray hat and a tattered brown coat. (7)His face was brown and wrinkled as if he had spent too much time in the sun. He looked down at the three cigarette butts. Then he looked off in the direction the children had gone. (8)He nodded his head as if he was thinking of some secret that only he knew. Then he turned and walked off in the opposite direction.

Part 4 Papa's Note

"Papa, we're home!" Miki said as she burst through the door. She didn't wait for an answer, but ran to her room, where she put Koko the lizard in a glass cage that had a small plant, a large rock, many snails, and a small turtle in a small pool of water at the bottom. Koko climbed to the top of the plant and looked around at his new home.

"(9)No, you don't!" Miki said, looking into the cage that was next to Koko's. It held a long skinny green snake that was watching Koko (10)closely. "Koko is not your dinner. He's our new friend." She moved the snake cage away from the lizard's cage.

"Okay, (11)everybody," she said, looking around her room at the lizard cage, the snake cage, a cage that held two rabbits, one that held a big black spider, one with five mice, one with small beetles, one with two frogs, and a jar with 23 tadpoles in water. "I will get all of your dinners in just a moment."

Miki walked to the kitchen, where Daisuke and Hide were looking at the table. It was set for three places and a large pot of steaming stew was sitting in the middle of everything. Daisuke reached down and picked up a piece of paper that was lying on one of the plates.

"Where's Papa?" Miki asked as she opened the refrigerator. She reached into the bottom and grabbed some plastic bags full of worms in dirt, various types of flies and small insects, and a couple of carrots and some lettuce.

"I wish you wouldn't keep your animal food in the fridge," said Hide. "It's pretty disgusting to look at."

"Animals have to eat, too, you know," said Miki as she walked back to her room.

"Look at (12)this," said Daisuke. He held out the piece of paper in his hand.

But Hide had his head in the refrigerator. "Look at (13)this," he said. He opened the door wide. "Papa made a ton of food and put it in freezer bags in the freezer. There is enough food here to (14)last us a week."

"Look here," said Daisuke, still holding out the paper. It had some writing on it in Papa's hand. Hide leaned closer. (15)It was very difficult to read as if it had been written in great haste. It said :

be back in a while
food in fridge

top dresser drawer

0922

don't tell anyone

stay together

don't worry if you can help it

"What does this mean?" asked Hide.

"I have no idea," said Daisuke.

He was interrupted by the sound of someone knocking loudly on the door.

Exercise A — Choose the correct answer.

1. How many cigarette butts did they find?
    a. One.
    b. Two.
    c. Three.
    d. Four.

2. Who had probably smoked in the forest?
    a. A man who got lost.
    b. A man wearing a gray hat and a brown coat.
    c. Someone Daisuke doesn't know.
    d. Someone Miki had seen before.

3. Daisuke returned home
    a. with Miki.
    b. with Miki and Hide.
    c. with Mike, Hide and Tetsu.
    d. with Mike, Hide, Tetsu and Father.

4. What did Miki do after she returned home?
   a. Put the lizard in a glass cage.
   b. Moved the snake cage away from the glass cage.
   c. Took some animal food out of the refrigerator.
   d. All of the above.

5. What did Daisuke and Hide find on the table in the kitchen?
   a. Three plates.
   b. Three plates and a pot of stew.
   c. Three plates, a pot of stew and a lot of frozen food.
   d. Three plates, a pot of stew and a piece of paper.

Exercise B Answer the following questions.

問1　下線部(1)(6)が何節であるかを指摘しなさい。
問2　下線部(2)(5)(10)(14)の品詞と意味を日本語で答えなさい。
問3　下線部(3)those old storiesとはどのような話か、日本語で説明しなさい。
問4　下線部(4)のandは何を結んでいるか指摘しなさい。
問5　下線部(7)(8)(15)を日本語に訳しなさい。
問6　下線部(9)で美樹がNo, you don't!と言った理由を日本語で説明しなさい。
問7　下線部(11)で美樹がeverybodyと呼びかけている動物をすべて日本語で指摘しなさい。
問8　下線部(12)(13)のthisはそれぞれ何を指しているか、日本語で答えなさい。

Grammar for Comprehension (問題)

　人が話をするとき、自分のまわりで起こったことや起こっていることをありのままに述べるのが普通ですが、ときどき、現実とは異なることを仮想することがありますね。このユニットでは、そうした場合に用いる「仮定法」について学習しましょう。

Questions

Q1 「明日の天気がよければ外出します」という場合の仮定と「天気がよければ、外出できるのに」という場合の仮定との違いがわかりますか？

Q2 次の文で「仮定法」が使われているのはどれでしょうか？

1. If he catches any kids on his land, they disappear and are never seen again.
2. I wish you wouldn't keep your animal food in the fridge.
3. He nodded his head as if he was thinking of some secret that only he knew.
4. His face was brown and wrinkled as if he had spent too much time in the sun.
5. It was very difficult to read as if it had been written in great haste.

Q3 「仮定法」の文の動詞や助動詞はどんな形をしていますか？

Check Your Answers

クラスでQuestionsに対する答えを確認してから、Exerciseの練習問題に進みなさい。Questionsについての詳しい説明は、解説を参照しなさい。

Exercise

次の中で仮定法の文がどれかを指摘し、仮定法が用いられている理由を説明しなさい。

1. I wish I had seen the look on that bully's face when he got bit.
2. It looks like someone was standing behind this tree watching us.
3. Don't worry if you can help it.
4. We are going to need more than that if he stays away very long.
5. Tetsu scratched at the door as if he wanted to go out.
6. If it bites me again, I'm going to call the police.
7. It is better if we stay here tonight.
8. If the police know we are here without any parents, they will take us away.

Grammar for Comprehension（解説）

1　仮定法とは？

　「仮定法」について誤解をしている人が多いようです。例えば、接続詞のifが出てくる文を見ると、それがすべて仮定法だと思ってはいないでしょうか？　Ｑ１の「明日の天気がよければ外出します」という文は、天気がよい場合とよくない場合に分けて、よい場合のことに言及しています。この英文は、"If it <u>is</u> fine tomorrow, I <u>will go</u> out." となりますね。

　Ｑ２の１番の文もIfで始まっていますが、仮定法の文ではありません。「彼が子どもを捕まえた」場合の話をしているのであって、その場合には捕まった子どもがいなくなってしまう、という事実に言及しているのです。このように、ほとんどの英文は現在・過去・未来の事実や予定について述べているのであり、これを表現するための述語動詞の形を「直説法」と呼んでいます。つまり、１番ではcatches, disappear, are seenと「直説法現在形」の動詞が用いられていますが、通常は単に「現在形」と言っているのです。こういうifを「場合のif」と呼んで区別するとよいでしょう。

　日本語では、さまざまな仮定の話をしますが、その中には「〜の場合」という以外に、Ｑ１の「天気がよければ、外出できるのに」のように、事実に反する仮定（＝仮想）も含まれています。英語では、これを直説法と厳密に区別し、仮定法を用いて "If the weather <u>were</u> fine, I <u>could go</u> out." と表現するのです。Ifの節は従属節ですから、前後を入れ替えて、"I <u>could go</u> out if the weather <u>were</u> fine." としても構いません。この下線を施した動詞・助動詞が「仮定法過去形」です。

　仮定法の「法」を英語ではmoodと言います。仮定法というのは、話し手・書き手が事実と反する想定をしたい気持ち（mood）になったときに用いる形式なのです。したがって、話し手・書き手の心の中には前提となる「事実」が存在するはずですね。天気の例では、現在の天気が（雨あるいは雪のため）悪くて外出できない状態にあることが前提で、それとは異なる状況を望む気持ちを表明しようと、仮定法を用いているのです。

2　仮定法の表現形式

　天気の例文のような仮定法を用いた典型的な英文には、ifを用いて仮定を示す部分（＝条件節）と、その結果を示す部分（＝帰結節）とがあり、帰結節では仮定法過去の助動詞（would, should, could, mightなど）が用いられます。

　Unit 2のReadingに出てきたIf the ghost story were true, something should happen underneath the water. という文（p.16）でも、If the ghost story were trueと「幽霊の話が本当なら」と仮定の話を始め、それを受けて、「何かが起こるはず」とsomething should happen underneath the waterと語っています。

　仮定法の文には、Ｑ２の２番〜５番のように、帰結節がなく条件節のみということもあります。２番では、「今後も冷蔵庫にエサを保存する」はずという前提で、そうしないことを願っています。３番〜５番では、事実が不明という前提で、「あたかも考えているかのように」「まるで陽に当たり過ぎたかのように」「大急ぎで書いたかのように」と想定しているのです。

補足１

　中学生のころ、I want 〜と言う代わりにI would like 〜と表現すると、「控え目」な気持ちを表すと習ったはずです。仮定法を用いた表現には、この場合のように条件節がないこともあります。話し手・書き手に「もしできることなら」という気持ち（mood）が働いているが、それを表現しないで結果だけを表したものと思ってよいでしょう。次の文では、Canの代わりにCouldを用いて、「ひょっとしたら」という気持ちを表しています。

　　Could it be an address?

補足２

　Ｑ２の５番では、as if以下に仮定法過去完了形が用いられています。「むずかしかった」と考えた時点よりも「前の時点」に起こったことを想定しているためです。as if it was writtenという仮定法過去形が、「時制の一致」でas if it had been writtenとなったのではありません。

　見かけ上、仮定法過去の動詞は直説法の過去と同じ形、仮定法過去完了の動詞は直説法の過去完了と同じ形をしていますね。「時制の一致」を適用すると混乱が生じることになります。そんな理由で、仮定法の文には「時制の一致」を適用しないのです。

Unit 6 倒置・挿入・省略

Let's Read a Mystery and Master Grammar

Vocabulary 次の語句の意味を確かめ、音声のあとについて発音しなさい。 Track 11

peephole [píːphòul] 名C （ドアなどの）のぞき穴
witch [wítʃ] 名C 魔女、魔法使い
shiver [ʃívə] 自動 〈寒さ・恐怖などで〉震える、ぶるっと身震いする
blueberry [blúːbèri] 名 ブルーベリー
put down：〈動物〉を（苦痛を与えずに）殺す
motion [móuʃən] 自動 〈～するように〉身ぶりで合図する
overly [óuvəli] 副 あまりにも、過度に
deal [díːl] 名C 取引、うまい話
sweetie [swíːti] 名 かわいい人
loosen [lúːsn] 他動 ゆるめる、解き放つ
grip [gríp] 名 しっかりつかむこと、握ること
strain [stréin] 自動 強く引っ張る
stop by：立ち寄る

Listening イラストを見ながら *"The Samurai Treasure"* の続きを音声で聞き、次の質問に答えなさい。 Track 12

問1　大輔は何をしているのですか？
問2　家の中には誰がいますか？
問3　このあと家の中から、誰がどんな順で出てきますか？

Reading 物語 *"The Samurai Treasure"* の続きを読み、下の設問に答えなさい。

Part 5 Four Visitors

"Who is it?" asked Hide.

Daisuke was looking through the peephole in the door. "It's the three witches," he said. "And Big Takuma is with them."

Tetsu was barking at the door. Daisuke pushed him back and opened the door.

There in the door light stood three old ladies with long gray hair flowing out of the hoods of their long overcoats. (1)Behind them, half hidden in the dark, stood Big Takuma, whose fat body filled out his blue school uniform, making him look like a huge blueberry on legs. He jumped back when he saw the dog.

"Keep that dog away from me!" Big Takuma shouted. "If it bites me again, I'm going to call the police and have him put down!"

The old lady closest to the door motioned for Takuma to be quiet. "Where is your father?" she asked in an overly sweet voice. "We need to talk to him about (2)something important."

Daisuke stepped outside and half closed the door behind him. He began to shiver in the cool night air. "Ah, he's … he's not here right now. He'll … ah … be back soon. Can I give him a message?"

"Not here?" the old lady looked back at her sisters with a puzzled expression on her face. "Where is he then? (3)He didn't go off and leave you poor children all alone, did he?" Her face twisted into a false look of pity and concern.

"No," said Daisuke. "He just stepped out to the, ah, the convenience store to get something for dinner. He'll be back soon. What do you want me to tell him?"

"I think he knows what we have to say," one of the sisters in the back said. "Tell him we have a very good business deal that he should take. (4)We'll give him a lot of money, to be sure, for that worthless piece of land behind your house." She stepped forward and reached out to touch Daisuke's face. "Oh, sweetie, (5)so much money to buy nice things for you and your brother and sister."

Daisuke stepped to one side before she could touch him. "I'll tell him, but I know his answer," he said. "That's our land. We won't sell."

The three old ladies laughed and moved in closer around Daisuke. Big Takuma moved in closer, too.

"But it's worthless land," said the closest old lady. "And (6)you kids could have so many nice things ...."

Big Takuma stepped forward and grabbed Daisuke by the shirt collar. "You really should sell," he said.

The door opened and Miki stepped out. "Where's Papa?" she said. "I can't find him anywhere! Oh, hello," she said when she saw the four visitors. "What are you doing here?"

"Miki, go back inside," Daisuke said, trying to loosen Big Takuma's grip on his shirt.

"Oh, look! It's the cute little girl," said one of the old ladies as she stepped closer. She held out something in her hand. "Look, I brought something nice for you; delicious sweet candy. Here, take it."

"Thanks," said Miki and she reached out her hand.

Daisuke pulled himself free of Big Takuma's grip and pulled back Miki's hand. "Thanks but she's not allowed, I'm afraid, to have candy before dinner," he said, pushing Miki back toward the door.

The door opened suddenly and Hide was there, holding Tetsu on a leash. The dog was straining against the chain and barking loudly. "Hello, Big Takuma," he said, moving toward the four visitors. "Do you remember your good friend Tetsu? He wants to play with you again."

The four visitors stepped back. Takuma jumped the farthest away.

"Thank you for coming to visit," Daisuke said, pushing his brother and sister and the dog back through the door. "I'll tell Father you stopped by," he said as he closed the door and locked it tight.

Exercise A   **Choose the correct answer.**

1. Who were the visitors?
    a. Takuma and his classmates.
    b. Takuma and three old ladies.
    c. Three witches with their dog.
    d. Father's friends in town.

2. Why did they come to Daisuke's house?
    a. To take Tetsu to the police station.
    b. To talk with Father about the forest.
    c. Because Tetsu had bitten and injured someone in town.
    d. Because they wanted to buy Daisuke's house.

3. Daisuke told them that
    a. his father had disappeared.
    b. the land behind his house was worthless.
    c. his family would be happy to get a lot of money from them.
    d. he would tell his father about their visit.

4. What did Miki do?
    a. She rceived candy from the visitors.
    b. She hid herself behind the front door.
    c. She stepped outside and spoke to the visitors.
    d. She brought Tetsu to frighten the visitors.

5. Daisuke
   a. tried to be good to the visitors.
   b. asked the visitors to come again.
   c. told Hide to put the leash on Tetsu.
   d. decided to search for his father.

Exercise B **Answer the following questions.**

問1　下線部(1)(3)(4)を日本語に訳しなさい。

問2　下線部(2)something important とはどのようなことですか、日本語で説明しなさい。

問3　下線部(5)の前に省略されている語句を補いなさい。

問4　下線部(6)は仮定法の帰結節です。どのような条件節を補うとよいでしょうか、英語で答えなさい。

Grammar for Comprehension（問題）

　英語は語順が重要な役割を果たす言語です。助動詞や動詞を主語の前に置くことによって疑問文であることを示すのは、その一例ですね。平叙文であっても、語順が変化することがあります。このユニットでは、普通の語順と異なる英文について学習しましょう。

Questions

Q1　次の各文は、通常の語順（文）とどんな点が異なるでしょうか？
   1. There in the door light stood three old ladies with long gray hair.
   2. Behind them, half hidden in the dark, stood Big Takuma.
   3. We'll give him a lot of money, to be sure, for that worthless piece of land.
   4. She's not allowed, I'm afraid, to have candy before dinner.
   5. "He's not here right now." "Not here?"

Q2　1番と2番の文を普通の語順に戻すと、どんな文になりますか？

Q3　5番の疑問文に省略された語句を補うと、どんな文になりますか？

✓ Check Your Answers

クラスでQuestionsに対する答えを確認してから、Exerciseの練習問題に進みなさい。Questionsについての詳しい説明は、解説を参照しなさい。

Exercise 1 次の文を普通の語順に戻しなさい。

1. Around it were long pink clouds that looked like cotton candy.
2. Near the edge of the clearing was a small pile of stones.
3. There in a tattered brown coat and a wrinkled old gray hat stood Old Man Yamada.
4. In the middle of it all stood the three Maeda sisters.
5. Behind him walked several policemen.

Exercise 2 次の下線部の省略を補って普通の文に書き換えなさい。

1. It said: <u>be back in a while</u>.
2. It said: <u>food in fridge</u>.
3. There is a little money here, <u>but not much</u>.
4. <u>Nothing</u> to worry about.
5. "Is it poisonous?" "No, but <u>this is</u>."

Grammar for Comprehension (解説)

1 倒置

英語の平叙文は「主語→述語動詞→その他の要素」という語順が普通ですが、Q1の1番や2番のように、動詞が主語の前に出ることがあります。それぞれ普通の語順は、Three old ladies with long gray hair stood <u>there in the door light</u>. Big Takuma stood <u>behind them, half hidden in the dark</u>. ですね。1番や2番の文では、下線部を文頭に出して強調しています。それにともなって、動詞stoodが主語の前に出たのです。

2　挿入

　文の途中で話し手・書き手の主張・意見・説明などを表したい場合には、その語句を挿入することになります。その結果、普通の語順とは異なる英文となるのです。Ｑ１の３番、４番では to be sure, I'm afraid という挿入句が見られますが、その前後にカンマがあるので容易に見分けがつくでしょう。

3　省略

　「省略」も普通の語順とは異なります。Ｑ１の５番では、相手が言った "He's not here right now." を疑問文にして、"Isn't he here right now?" あるいは "Is he not here right now?" と聞き返してもいいのですが、同じ語句を繰り返すのを避けて、ポイントとなる not, here だけを残して発言したのです。

　Unit 2に出てきた "What about the treasure?" [p.15] は、"What do you think about the treasure?" という文の省略と考えられます。How about ～? Why not? if possible のような慣用句も同様です。また、Unit 5の最後に出てきたメモの書き出し [p.42] は、"I'll be back in a while" とすべきところを "be back in a while" と省略してありました。会話文や私的な手紙（メモ）では、こうした現象がよく起こるのです。

補足

　疑問文では、助動詞や動詞が主語の前に出るのが普通ですね。平叙文であっても、There is/are ～構文では、be動詞の後ろに主語がきます。また、次の文のように、伝達動詞 said の主語が名詞の場合、倒置が起こりやすいのですが、主語が代名詞のときには普通の語順になります。

　　　"But it's worthless land," said the closest old lady.
　　　　cf. "But it's worthless land," she said.

Unit 7

5W1H

Vocabulary 次の語句の意味を確かめ、音声のあとについて発音しなさい。 Track 13

scratch ［skrǽtʃ］ 他動 ひっかく
ladle ［léidl］ 他動 〈スープなど〉をよそう、〈他の容器に〉移す
figure out：～を解決する、解き明かす
dresser ［drésə］ 名Ⓒ 鏡付き化粧だんす
drawer ［drɔ́ːə］ 名Ⓒ 引出し
loose change ［lúːs tʃéindʒ］ 名Ⓤ （ポケット・財布の中の）小銭
wallet ［wάlit］ 名Ⓒ （主に男性用の）札入れ、財布
take turns ～ing：交代で～する
get ～ off：～を送り出す
split ［splít］ 他動 分ける、離す
household chores ［háushòuld tʃɔ́ːz］ 名 家事、家庭の雑用

Listening 次ページのイラストを見ながら "The Samurai Treasure" の続きを音声で聞き、次の質問に答えなさい。 Track 14

問1 上のイラストで、子どもたちが食べているのは何でしょう？
問2 下のイラストで、大輔と秀典が読んでいるのは何ですか？
問3 その中のどんな内容について話し合っているのでしょうか？
問4 お父さんは戻ってきましたか？

Reading 物語 *"The Samurai Treasure"* の続きを読み、下の設問に答えなさい。

Part 6 Number 0922

After a while the dog stopped barking and scratching at the door. The three children sat down at the table and began their dinner.

"I still don't know why I couldn't take the candy," said Miki.

"Don't ever, EVER take anything those people give you," said Daisuke.

"Why not?" said Miki as she ladled out some stew into her bowl. "They seem like nice old ladies."

"(1)Things are not always what they seem," said Hide.

"No?" said Miki. "(2)Well, this seems like good stew. Is it?"

"Yes," said Hide. "Papa made it, so it's good."

Miki had a taste. "Yes, it is good," she said. "And Papa seems to be gone somewhere. Where is he?"

Daisuke and Hide looked at each other. Hide motioned his head toward the note which Papa had written. "What is Papa doing?" he whispered to his brother. "And 0922. What does it mean?"

"I don't know," Daisuke whispered back. "I don't know."

The next day Papa still had not come back. It was a Saturday, so the three children didn't have to go to school. There was plenty of food in the house and all three kids knew how to cook, so they were okay for now. (3)While Miki played with her animals in her room, Daisuke and Hide tried to figure out the message on Papa's note.

The two boys looked in Papa's top dresser drawer and found nothing there except some loose change, some handkerchiefs and Papa's wallet.

"Maybe this is what Papa wanted us to find," said Hide. He took the wallet and looked inside. "There is a little money here, but not much."

"We are going to need more than that if he stays away very long," said Daisuke. "What is Papa doing? What does the number 0922 mean?"

"It's too short to be a phone number," said Hide. "Could it be an address?"

"An address needs a street name," said Daisuke. "Maybe it's a code."

"A code?" asked Hide.

"Yeah. A code," said Daisuke. "You know, like the letter A is number 1, B is 2, and so on."

"So (4)that would make this zero, IBB. What letter is zero?" asked Hide.

"I don't know," said Daisuke.

Part 7 Life Without Papa

Several days went by and the children did their best to lead normal lives. Daisuke got his brother and sister up and off to school in the morning. At the end of the day, he hurried from his high school to meet Miki at the elementary school and Hide at the junior high so that they could walk home together. They took turns cooking, washing dishes and washing the clothes. When Miki asked where Papa was, the two boys told her he was away on business and would be back soon.

"Maybe we should tell the police Papa is missing," said Hide one night.

"The note said, 'Don't tell anyone,'" said Daisuke. "Besides, if the police know we are here without any parents, they will take us away, split us up and put us in (5)a government home. We should stay together. Don't tell anyone Papa is away. We will be okay."

Exercise A   **Choose the correct answer.**

1. What did the three children do?
    a. They began to quarrel before they had dinner.
    b. They sat at the table to eat what their father had made.
    c. They had dinner together and took a hot bath.
    d. They tried to find out where their father had gone.

2. Who knows where their father has gone?
    a. Daisuke.
    b. Hide.
    c. Miki.
    d. None of them.

3. What did Daisuke and Hide find the next day?
    a. what the number 0992 meant.
    b. their father's wallet with some money.
    c. a lot of money in their father's dresser.
    d. another note hidden in their father's room.

4. Who did the household chores?
    a. All three children.
    b. Only Daisuke.
    c. Daisuke and Hide.
    d. Hide and Miki.

5. What will the children do?
   a. Try to live as they used to.
   b. Ask their neighbor for help.
   c. Tell the police about their father.
   d. Stay home and never go out.

Exercise B Answer the following questions.

問1 下線部(1)(3)を日本語に訳しなさい。

問2 下線部(2)のように美樹が言ったのはなぜでしょうか、日本語で説明しなさい。

問3 下線部(4)のthatとはどうすることですか、日本語で説明しなさい。また、thisは何を指していますか。

問4 下線部(5)で大輔がa government homeと言っているのは、何のことだと思われますか、日本語で答えなさい。

Grammar for Comprehension（問題）

5W1Hということばを聞いたことがあるでしょうか。このユニットでは、このことばに注目して学習を進めます。まず、次の質問に答えましょう。

Questions

Q1 5W1Hの5つのW、1つのHはそれぞれ何でしょうか？

Q2 次の各文の下線部について、その用法を説明できますか？
   1. I still don't know why I couldn't take the candy.
   2. What letter is zero?
   3. Hide motioned his head toward the note which Papa had written.
   4. Maybe this is what Papa wanted us to find.
   5. All three kids knew how to cook.

Check Your Answers

クラスでQuestionsに対する答えを確認してから、Exerciseの練習問題に進みなさい。Questionsについての詳しい説明は、解説を参照しなさい。

Exercise 次の文中の下線を施した5W1Hの用法を説明しなさい。

1. Then he went with the few Kinoshitas who were still alive and hid in the forest.
2. I see where you got the name.
3. Tetsu lowered his head and sniffed at the spot where the cigarettes lay.
4. Miki walked to the kitchen, where Daisuke and Hide were looking at the table.
5. Things are not always what they seem.
6. When Miki asked where Papa was, the two boys told her he was away on business.
7. "What's for lunch?" Miki asked when they got home.
8. Why in the last few months have they wanted our land so badly?
9. Let's see what they were doing there last night.
10. He led them to his car which was parked down the road.

Grammar for Comprehension（解説）

1　5W1Hとは？

Who, When, Where, What, Why, Howという6つの単語の頭文字をとって、5W1Hと呼んでいます。「だれが、いつ、どこで、何を」するのか／したのかは、話の内容を構成する重要な要素で、その理由（なぜ）や展開（どのように）に関心が向けられることから、新聞の記事を書いたり、プレゼンテーションをする場合の心得となっています。***"The Samurai Treasure"*** を読み進む際にExercise Aに取り組んでいますが、この物語の5W1Hを確かめるための問題となっているのです。

これら6つの単語は、疑問詞としてWh-疑問文に用いられるのはもちろんのこと、

間接疑問文の先頭に立つほか、関係代名詞や関係副詞として重要な働きをします。whenは接続詞としても頻繁に用いられ、whatとhowは感嘆文の冒頭に現れます。さらに、what to ～, how to ～ など、不定詞と結びついた用法もありますね。

2　間接疑問文

Q2の1番のwhy以下は間接疑問文です。Why couldn't I take candy?という疑問文をknowの目的語の位置に入れる際に、why以下を平叙文の語順にして名詞節としたのです。2番目の文をI wonderの後ろに入れて間接疑問文にすれば、I wonder what letter zero is.となりますね。なお、この疑問詞whatは名詞letterの前に置かれているので、厳密には、疑問形容詞となっています。

3　関係代名詞

関係代名詞は、もともと2つの文であったものを、関係代名詞を「交わり」にして、1つの文にする際に用いられるものです。例えば、Q2の3番の文 ［＝(c)］は、［交わりの図］にあるように、(a) Hide motioned his head toward the note. と (b) Papa had written it. を1文にしたものです。(c)では、もとの2文に共通するthe note = it のうち、前者が先行詞（被修飾語）となり、後者が関係代名詞となって(a)と(b)を仲介する結び目となっています。したがって、関係代名詞は先行詞を修飾する語句（＝形容詞節）の先頭に立ち、その形容詞節中で主語・目的語・補語または前置詞の目的語のいずれかとなっているはずです。

［交わりの図］

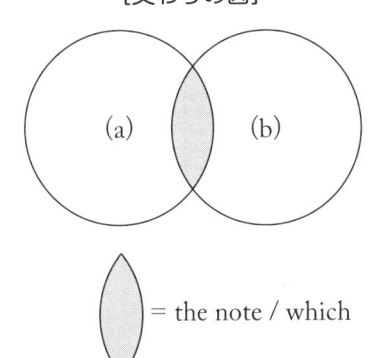

(a) Hide motioned his head toward the note.
＋
(b) Papa had written it.

＝ (c) Hide motioned his head toward the note which Papa had written.

＝ the note / which

4　関係代名詞what

関係代名詞whatには、Q2の4番のように先行詞がありません。先行詞を用いて表現すれば、Maybe this is the thing which Papa wanted us to find. となるでしょう。このように、関係代名詞のwhatは、漠然と「～というもの」「～という人」などの意味を表したいときに用います。間接疑問文のようにも見えることもありますが、先行詞を用いる必要がないので、便利なことばですね。

5　関係副詞

関係副詞も同様に2つの文の結び目となりますが、関係副詞という名前からもわかるように、関係副詞以下の節では副詞として位置づけられます。例えば、**"The Samurai Treasure"** の冒頭に出てきたThis is the place where the Kinoshita clan made their last stand. は、(a) This is the place. と (b) The Kinoshita clan made their last stand at the place. を1文にしたと考えられます。

2つの文に共通するのはthe placeですね。(a)のthe placeを先行詞とし、(b)のthe placeを関係代名詞whichに置き換えてThis is the place at which the Kinoshita clan made their last stand. とすることもできるのですが、(b)のat the place (=there) を関係副詞のwhereに変えて1つの文にしたのです。［交わりの図］にあてはめると、次のようになります。

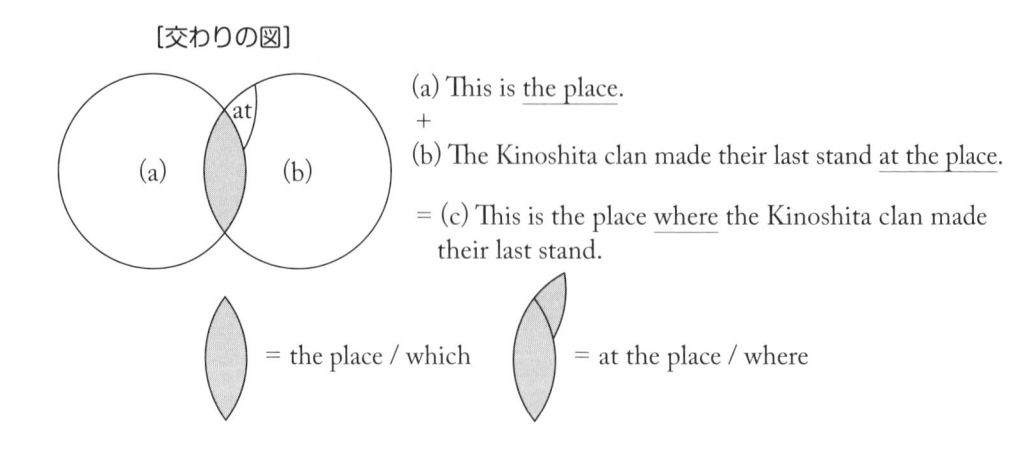

［交わりの図］

(a) This is the place.
+
(b) The Kinoshita clan made their last stand at the place.

= (c) This is the place where the Kinoshita clan made their last stand.

= the place / which　　= at the place / where

6　疑問詞＋不定詞

Q2の5番は、All three kids knew how they should cook. の下線部を不定詞を用い

て言い換えた文で、「どのように料理するべきかということ」つまり「料理の仕方」という意味になります。同様に考えれば、what to cook, when to cook, where to cook は、それぞれ「何を料理すべき」「いつ料理すべき」「どこで料理すべき」という意味になりますね。

補足 1

関係代名詞の目的格は省略することができるので、例えばＱ２の３番の文は、Hide motioned his head toward the note Papa had written. となります。このように省略された結果、先行詞のすぐ後ろに修飾語句が続くことになり、接触節（contact clause）と呼ばれます。***"The Samurai Treasure"*** では、これまでに以下のような接触節がありました。

> The only treasure I have is you, your brother and your sister. [Unit 2]
> Daisuke threw down the one he had in his hand with disgust. [Unit 5]
> Don't ever, EVER take anything those people give you. [Unit 7]

補足 2

関係副詞の場合、先行詞がよく省略されます。where は「場所」、when は「時」、why は「理由」、how は「方法」を表す言葉が先行詞となるため、省略しても理解できることが多いからです。***"The Samurai Treasure"*** の次の文では、howやwhereの先行詞が省略されていました。

> That is (the way) how the hot spring came to exist. [Unit 2]
> A tall man walked over to (the place) where the cigarettes lay. [Unit 5]

逆に、以下の文のように、関係副詞のほうが省略されることもあります。

> Then he looked off in the direction (where) the children had gone. [Unit 5]

補足 3

関係代名詞・関係副詞には、先行詞を後ろから修飾する「制限用法」のほか、Exercise の４番のような「非制限用法」あるいは「継続用法」と呼ばれる使い方もあります。関係代名詞や関係副詞の前にカンマがあるのが特徴です。この４番の文では、「そして、そこ（＝台所）で」という意味になります。

耳に聞こえる英語の音

　島田幸子さんは、自分の名前をローマ字で書くとき、小学校では"Simada Satiko"と習っていたのに、中学校に入って英語の授業を受けると、"Shimada Sachiko"と綴るようにと言われました。なぜでしょうか？

　小学校のときは「訓令式」、中学校では「ヘボン式」という表記法にしたがっているからです。訓令式は、日本語の五十音図を念頭に考えられたものですが、ヘボン式は日本語の本来の音を発音するのに適した表記法なのです。"Simada"のように綴ると、冒頭の"Si"は［si］（＝スィ）と発音され、日本語の「シ」とは異なる音となってしまいます。"Satiko"の"ti"も日本語の「チ」ではなく、［ti］（＝ティ）と発音されてしまいます。

　このローマ字表記法を考案したのは、江戸時代の末期にアメリカからやってきたJames Hepburnという宣教師で、彼の苗字をとって「ヘボン式」としたのです。彼の苗字は有名な女優であったAudrey Hepburnと同じなのですが、なぜ「ヘップバーン」ではないのでしょう？　それは、［hépbə:n］と破裂音の［p］と［b］が続くため、前の［p］がしっかりと発音されず、聞こえにくくなった結果、日本人の耳には「ヘボン」と聞こえたからです。

　この例のように、明治時代に外国語が日本に入ってきましたが、日本人の耳に聞こえたようにカタカナにした外来語がたくさんでき上がりました。以前、小麦粉のことを「メリケン粉」と言っていました。横浜や神戸の港を「メリケン波止場」と呼んでいました。どんな英語を聞いて「メリケン」としたかがわかるでしょうか？　これは、Americanという英語を聞いてカタカナにしてしまった結果です。［əmérikən］と最初の［ə］が曖昧母音のため、日本人の耳には聞こえにくく、消えてしまったのです。

　パイナップルは、英語でpineappleと綴ります。松（pine）の木の実（＝松かさ、まつぼっくり）に形が似ている果物（appleは果物の代表）ということで、そのように名づけられたそうです。日本人が「パイナップル」と言っているのは、pineappleの発音を聞いて、そのままカタカナにしたからです。［páinæpl］の［n］と［æ］がつながって［næ］と発音されるため、「パイン・アップル」ではなく「パイ（ン）ナップル」と聞こえるのです。

　日本人は視覚型民族と言われており、文字が邪魔をして英語の発音を間違えたり、正確に聞き取れないことがあります。明治時代の日本人のように、耳に聞こえてくる音を大切にすると、英語がよく聞き取れるようになるかもしれません。

Unit 8 接続詞の用法

Let's Read a Mystery and Master Grammar

Vocabulary 次の語句の意味を確かめ、音声のあとについて発音しなさい。 Track 15

berry ［béri］ 名C ベリー〔イチゴの類などの核のない食用小果実〕

extensive ［iksténsiv］ 形 広大な

brick ［brík］ 名C レンガ

pull up：〈車が〉〈…に〉止まる、横付けになる

unload ［ʌ̀nlóud］ 他動 〈人・積荷〉をおろす

lick ［lík］ 他動 〈人・動物が〉〈物〉をなめる、なめて食べる

bulldozer ［búldòuzə］ 名C ブルドーザー

backhoe ［bǽkhou］ 名C バックホー〔長いアームの先にシャベルがついた掘削機；その掘削装置〕

catch one's breath：息をのむ、ひと息つく

run into ～：〈人〉に偶然出会う

whistle ［hwísl］ 自動 口笛を吹く、口笛で合図する

That is a good one.：うまいこと言うね。やったね。

PIN number：暗証番号

whine ［hwáin］ 自動 〈犬が〉くんくん鳴く

collide ［kəláid］ 自動 衝突する

Listening イラストを見ながら *"The Samurai Treasure"* の続きを音声で聞き、次の質問に答えなさい。

問1　上のイラストに見えるのは誰の家の塀でしょうか？
問2　そこで二人は何を目撃しましたか？
問3　その後、帰宅してから誰かが再び外出しました。誰が何をしに出かけたのですか？
問4　下のイラストで二人は何（誰）を見ているのですか？

Reading 物語 *"The Samurai Treasure"* の続きを読み、下の設問に答えなさい。

Part 8 The Maeda House

The weekend came around again and they ate the last of the food Papa had left for breakfast.

"Good," said Miki. "I'm tired of eating soup!"

They had already spent the little amount of money in Papa's wallet for rice and fruit juice. The boys thought about going into the forest and picking berries for food. But they were sure the number 0922 was somehow important. They made a plan. (1)Daisuke took Miki into town to get some ice cream with the last of their money, while Hide went searching along the city streets for an address that had 0922 in it.

As they were returning home, Daisuke and Miki walked past the Maeda house where the three old sisters lived. It was a huge house surrounded by an extensive garden and a brick wall. As they walked by, several large trucks pulled up in front of the house. Many big strong-looking men got out of the trucks and began unloading a lot of heavy machines into the yard.

"What are they doing?" asked Miki as she licked the top of her chocolate ice cream cone.

"I don't know, but it can't be good," said Daisuke. He saw a bulldozer with a backhoe drive off the back of a truck. "It looks like they are planning on doing some digging," he said.

As they (2)neared their house on the edge of town, they saw Hide running after them as fast as he could run. After he reached them, he stopped to catch his breath before he could talk.

"I just ran into Big Takuma," said Hide. "He was standing on the street corner, smoking cigarettes. He grabbed me and started shouting crazy things at me," he said.

"What did he say?" asked Daisuke.

"He said, 'You stupid Kinoshitas! You think you are so important because you have (3)all that land. Well, we're going to take it away from you. It's going to be ours!'" said Hide. "And then he acted like he was going to burn me with his cigarette, but I whistled for Tetsu to come and Takuma got scared and ran away."

"Oh," laughed Daisuke, "so Tetsu saved you once again!"

"No," said Hide. "Tetsu wasn't there. I just whistled and Big Takuma thought he was coming and ran away."

All three of them laughed until their stomachs hurt.

"(4)That was a good one," said Daisuke.

"What's for lunch?" Miki asked when they got home.

Daisuke and Hide looked at each other and couldn't answer. There was no more food in the house. "I don't know" said Hide. "(5)I spent all morning trying to figure out what the number 0922 means."

"0922?" said Miki. "Oh, that's easy."

"What do you mean that's easy?" asked Daisuke.

"That's the PIN number for Papa's cash card," said Miki.

"What?" asked Hide. "How do you know that?"

"(6)I watch every time he uses the card to get money," said Miki. "He thinks I don't see, but I do."

"The cash card!" said both boys at once. Hide ran to the dresser and got Papa's wallet. Inside he found the cash card. He ran off to the nearest convenience store and came back with a bag full of sandwiches, fried chicken, potato chips and chocolate candy.

Part 9   Old Man Yamada

Tetsu was chewing on a piece of fried chicken, when he suddenly sat up and ran to the front door. He whined and scratched at the door as if he wanted to go out.

"What's wrong, Tetsu?" asked Hide. "Is someone out there? Did Papa come back?" He walked to the door and looked out of the peephole.

"Ooh, ooh," he said. "Daisuke, come here and look out of the window. But do it carefully. Look over there. Someone is hiding behind that tree across the street."

Daisuke stood to one side of the window and slowly pulled back one corner of the curtain. He peeked out.

"Old Man Yamada!" he said. "What's he doing out there?"

"He looks like he's watching our house," said Hide. "You don't suppose that he's working with the Maedas, do you?"

Daisuke shook his head. "What is going on?" asked Hide. "Why in the last few months have they wanted our land so badly? They own everything else around here. What can they want with our little piece of forest?"

"I have no idea," said Daisuke. "And what does Old Man Yamada have to do with all of this? Why don't the Maedas take Old Man Yamada's land? He owns more than we do."

"Because he's the only person around here who is scarier than (7)they are," said Hide, and the two boys laughed quietly.

"Do you think the stories about him are true?" asked Hide. "They say any kids who wander onto his property disappear and are never seen again."

"Oh, come on," said Daisuke. "You don't believe that stuff, do you? He's just an old guy who keeps to himself."

Exercise A **Choose the correct answer.**

1. Daisuke and Miki
    a. went to town to visit the Maedas.
    b. went into the forest to pick burries.
    c. saw Takuma grabing Hide and shouting at him.
    d. saw Hide running at full speed toward them.

2. Hide
    a. tried in vain to find a street address with the number 0922.
    b. ran into Takuma and started fighting with him.
    c. was saved by Tetsu before Takuma could hurt him.
    d. bought some ice cream for Miki and himself.

3. What was happening around the Maeda house?
    a. A bulldozer was digging a big hole in front of the house.
    b. A lot of men were bringing machines into the yard.
    c. Several trucks collided into one another near the house.
    d. The brick wall was being broken down.

4. The number 0922 turned out to be

    a. a telephone number.

    b. a house number.

    c. a cash card number.

    d. a bank account number.

5. Daisuke and Hide

    a. found Old Man Yamada standing near their house.

    b. ordered Tetsu not to bark at Old Man Yamada.

    c. asked Old Man Yamada not to watch their house.

    d. thought Old Man Yamada was working with the Maedas.

Exercise B Answer the following questions.

問1　下線部(1)(5)(6)を日本語に訳しなさい。

問2　下線部(2)の品詞と意味を指摘しなさい。

問3　下線部(3)all that landとはどこのことですか、日本語で答えなさい。

問4　下線部(4)That was a good oneのThatが指す内容を簡潔な日本語で答えなさい。

問5　下線部(7)のtheyは誰（何）を指していますか、日本語で答えなさい。

Grammar for Comprehension（問題）

　接続詞は語と語、句と句、節と節をつなぐ役割を果たしますが、何をどのようにつなぐのかは書き手（話し手）の判断によります。このユニットでは、従属接続詞の役割について考えてみましょう。

Questions

Q1　次の各文に使われている接続詞を指摘することができますか？

    1. As they were returning home, Daisuke and Miki walked past the Maeda house.

2. After he reached them, he stopped to catch his breath before he could talk.
3. You think you are so important because you have all that land.
4. It looks like they are planning on doing some digging.
5. I watch every time he uses the card to get money.

Q2 1番の文をDaisuke and Mikiで始まる文に書き換えることができますか？

✓ Check Your Answers

クラスでQuestionsに対する答えを確認してから、Exerciseの練習問題に進みなさい。Questionsについての詳しい説明は、解説を参照しなさい。

Exercise 次の文中の接続詞を指摘しなさい。

1. Daisuke took Miki into town to get some ice cream with the last of their money, while Hide went searching along the city streets for an address that had 0922 in it.
2. He acted like he was going to burn me with his cigarette.
3. All three of them laughed until their stomachs hurt.
4. "What's for lunch?" Miki asked when they got home.
5. You don't suppose that he's working with the Maedas, do you?
6. He's the only person around here who is scarier than they are.
7. She had stopped screaming the second she saw who the zombie really was.
8. I've known those three sisters since we were in kindergarten together.

Grammar for Comprehension（解説）

1 英文を拡大する手段

Unit 2で、動詞の働きに注目して英文の構造を分類すると、5つの文型になることを確認しました。これは、1つの主語（S）と1つの述語動詞（V）から成り立つ

ている「単文」レベルでの分類です。また、不定詞や動名詞は句レベルで文を長くするので、構造上は単文を保持します。

これに対して、接続詞は節レベルで文を長くすることが多く、2つのSとVが登場すると、「重文」「複文」と呼ばれる構造を形成することになります。そのほか、英文を拡大する手段として、Unit 7で学習した5W1Hの関係代名詞や関係副詞が活躍します。

2 等位接続詞と従属接続詞の違い

Unit 4で見たandは、等位接続詞の代表でした。等位接続詞は、語と語、句と句、節と節を結びます。しかも、結ばれる順序による序列はあるものの、語句や節は対等の関係にあります。一方、従属接続詞は、語や句を結ぶことはなく、節と節を主従の関係に結びつけます。

例えば、Q1の1番の文では、接続詞Asで始まる語群は、主節Daisuke and Miki walked past the Maeda houseに対して従属節の位置を占めています。主従の関係は語順とは関係がないので、この文の主節と従属節を入れ替えて、Daisuke and Miki walked past the Maeda house as they were returning home.としても、まったく同じ意味となります。

これからもわかるように、従属接続詞は従属節の先頭に立って、文中を移動することができるのです。この点が、等位接続詞との最大の違いですね。2つの節が等位接続詞で結ばれた場合を「重文」、従属接続詞で結ばれた場合を「複文」と呼ぶ理由もここにあるのです。

3 代表的な従属接続詞

Q1の2番の文ではAfterとbeforeが、3番の文ではbecauseが従属接続詞として使われていますね。このほか、***"The Samurai Treasure"***に出てきた代表的な従属接続詞には、以下のようなものがあります。

> They say that the ghost of Samurai Daisuke still guards the treasure. [Unit 2]
> If the ghost story were true, something should happen underneath the water. [Unit 2]
> Since your mother died, the only treasure I have is you, your brother and your sister. [Unit 2]

4　注意すべき従属接続詞

　Q1の4番目の文には、likeという語が見られます。***"The Samurai Treasure"*** のPart 2にあった long pink clouds that looked like the cotton candy［p.32］のlikeは前置詞ですが、この4番の文のlikeは接続詞です。5番ではevery timeが「〜するたびに」という接続詞として用いられています。従属接続詞には、このような特殊な接続詞や用法があるので、気をつけましょう。

補足1

　Unit 1で「1つの単語がいつも同じ役割を果たすとは限りません」「それぞれの語が文中でどのような役割を果たしているのかを見きわめる必要がある」と述べました。**4** の「注意すべき従属接続詞」で触れたlikeは、動詞・前置詞・接続詞のほか、次のように名詞としても用いられます。

　　Here is a list of my likes and dislikes.　（私の好き嫌いのリストですよ）

補足2

　"The Samurai Treasure" のPart 9の冒頭に、Tetsu was chewing on a piece of fried chicken, when he suddenly sat up and ran to the front door. という文［p.68］がありました。このwhenは接続詞のように見えますが、関係副詞の非制限用法（継続用法）です。次のように、and then と言い換えられます。

Tetsu was chewing on a piece of fried chicken, and then he suddenly sat up and ran to the front door.

Unit 9

Thatの用法

Vocabulary 次の語句の意味を確かめ、音声のあとについて発音しなさい。 Track 17

go (and) do：～しに行く［go see（見に行く）のように、andは省略されることがある］

check out ～：～を調べる

zombie［zámbi］名C ゾンビ

take a bite out of ～：～をひと口かじる

choke［tʃóuk］他動 息苦しくさせる

deed［díːd］名C 不動産譲渡証書

property［prápəti］名C 地所、不動産

let go of ～：～から手を離す

brush［brʌ́ʃ］他動 ～を払いのける

poisonous［pɔ́izənəs］形 有毒な

bruise［brúːz］名C すり傷、打撲傷

sore［sɔ́ə］形 ひりひりする

get to do：～する機会を得る

kidnap［kídnæp］他動 誘拐する

Listening イラストを見ながら *"The Samurai Treasure"* の続きを音声で聞き、次の質問に答えなさい。 (Track 18)

問1　ここはどこですか？
問2　大輔と秀典はなぜここにやって来たのですか？
問3　ここに隠れていたのは誰でしたか？
問4　この後、どんなことが起こりましたか？

Reading 物語 *"The Samurai Treasure"* の続きを読み、下の設問に答えなさい。

Part 10　Big Takuma

That night Daisuke was awakened by Hide pulling on his arm.

"Come on!" said Hide. "Come and look out the back window!"

He pulled Daisuke to the back of the house. "Look," he said, "back in the forest."

(1)Daisuke looked out of the back window and could just make out through the trees some faint lights and shadows moving in the forest. "Someone is back there in the woods," he said.

"We should go see who it is," said Hide.

"No!" said Daisuke. "It is better if we stay here tonight. We can check it out in the morning."

They both jumped when they heard Miki screaming. They ran to Miki's room and turned on the light. The first thing they noticed was that the window was wide open. Miki was sitting on her bed screaming.

"What is it, Miki?" asked Daisuke.

"A zombie!" screamed Miki. "It came in through the window!"

They heard the sound of laughing. Big Takuma stepped out of the shadow in the corner of the room. "That's a good one," he said. "Zombie! Ha-ha-ha!"

"What are you doing here?" shouted Hide. "You can't come into our house (2)like that!" He turned and whistled. "Tetsu!" he shouted. "Tetsu! Come and take another bite out of Big Takuma!"

Big Takuma only laughed harder. "That stupid dog is never going to bite anybody again," he said.

"What did you do?" asked Hide. "Where is my dog?" He ran at Takuma and tried to throw a punch, but Big Takuma reached out one huge hand and knocked him to one side.

Daisuke ran forward to help Hide, but Big Takuma grabbed him by the throat and began to choke him.

"Now," he said. "(3)I want you to tell me where your father keeps that piece of paper that says you own the land. The deed to the property. I want to see it."

Daisuke struggled to pull Takuma's hand from his throat. "I don't know about any paper!" he said. "Let go of me!"

"You don't have it, do you?" asked Big Takuma. "You don't really own the land at all. My family checked at the city office and you don't have any record that you own that land, do you?"

"I have something else." Everyone turned to see Miki standing quietly next to Big Takuma. (4)No one had noticed that she had stopped screaming the second she saw who the zombie really was.

"Yeah?" said Big Takuma. "What do you have, little girl?"

"This," said Miki. She stepped forward and laid a green snake over Big Takuma's shoulder.

"Ahhhh!" screamed Big Takuma. He jumped and ran screaming to the window. "What is that?" he shouted. He brushed the snake off his shoulder. "Is it poisonous?"

"No," said Miki. "But this is." She ran up to Takuma and placed a giant spider on his face.

Big Takuma screamed again, threw the spider off his face and jumped out of the window. They could hear him screaming as he ran away down the street.

Daisuke and Hide rubbed the bruises and sore spots on their bodies as they laughed. "Was it really poisonous?" asked Daisuke.

"No," said Miki. "It's too bad he left before he got to meet Koko." She held up the lizard for them to see. "Ko-ko!" it said. "Ko-ko!" (5)<u>The two brothers walked up on either side of Miki and hugged her as close as big brothers could.</u>

"Hey, kids," the three children jumped and turned toward the window. There in a tattered brown coat and a wrinkled old gray hat stood Old Man Yamada looking in at them.

"Hurry up!" he said. "And get into my car!"

Exercise A — Choose the correct answer.

1. Big Takuma
   a. was found to be smoking secretly in the woods.
   b. came into Miki's room through the window.
   c. brought some creatures into the Kinoshita house.
   d. was scared by Tetsu and ran away.

2. Miki
   a. saw a zombie coming into the room in her dream.
   b. screamed when she heard someone opening the window.
   c. put a snake over Big Takuma's shoulder.
   d. drove away Big Takuma with a poisonous spider.

3. Which of the following is correct?
   a. Hide tried to punch Big Takuma in vain.
   b. Daisuke knocked Big Takuma to one side.
   c. Big Takuma caught both Hide and Daisuke by the neck.
   d. The three boys made a big fight and were badly injured.

4. Why did Big Takuma come to the Kinoshita house?
    a. Because he wanted to make friends with the Kinoshitas.
    b. Because he was ordered by his grandmother to kidnap Miki.
    c. To return the insult Hide had made earlier that day.
    d. To get a document which shows the legal owner of the woods.

5. What might have happened to Tetsu? Give your guess.
    a. Big Takuma had done something bad to Tetsu.
    b. Old Man Yamada had taken Tetsu into the woods.
    c. Tetsu had found some strangers and chased after them.
    d. The children's father had returned to take Tetsu with him.

Exercise B　Answer the following questions.

問1　下線部(1)(3)(4)(5)を日本語に訳しなさい。

問2　下線部(2)like that とはどのようにしてということですか、日本語で説明しなさい。

Grammar for Comprehension（問題）

英語を聞いたり読んだりすると必ずと言っていいほど出てくる単語の1つにthatがあります。このユニットでは、thatの用法に的を絞って学習します。では、次の質問の答えを考えてみましょう。

Questions

Q1　次の各文中のthatの用法を説明できますか？

1. You can't come into our house like that!
2. That stupid dog is never going to bite anybody again.
3. I want you to tell me where your father keeps that piece of paper that says you own the land.
4. No one had noticed that she had stopped screaming.

5. Daisuke hurried to meet Miki at the elementary school so that they could walk home together.

Q2 3番の文では、どこかにthatが省略されています。どこでしょうか？

✔ Check Your Answers

クラスでQuestionsに対する答えを確認してから、Exerciseの練習問題に進みなさい。Questionsについての詳しい説明は、解説を参照しなさい。

Exercise 次の文中のthatの用法を指摘しなさい。

1. Daisuke is a name that has been in our family for a long time.
2. The first thing they noticed was that the window was wide open.
3. You don't have any record that you own that land, do you?
4. I am sorry that we are a family that is 'land rich and money poor.'
5. He's going to be a little mad that we stayed here this late anyway.
6. This little forest is the only piece of land that they don't own in the area.
7. Tell him that we have a very good business deal that he should take.
8. The family of the Daimyo that Samurai Daisuke fought for gave them to us as a gift.

Grammar for Comprehension（解説）

1　指示代名詞（指示形容詞）that

指示代名詞のthatは遠くにある人や物を指すときに用いられますが、Q1の1番のように、その場の状況で話し手・聞き手にわかっている内容を漠然と指したり、すでに述べたことを指すこともあります。また、2番のThat stupid dogのように名詞の前に置かれると指示形容詞となります。

② 関係代名詞 that

　関係代名詞 who, whose, whom, which のうちの whose を除くすべての関係代名詞に代わって that を用いることができます。ときには、関係副詞の when, where, how, why の代わりもするほどです。Ｑ１の３番で下線を施した that は、which に代わって用いられた関係代名詞（主格）ですね。that が好んで用いられる場合もあるのですが、厳密なルールがあるわけではありません。英文解釈の際には、that の文中での役割が関係代名詞か接続詞かを見きわめることのほうが重要となります。

　目的格の関係代名詞は省略できるのでしたね。Exercise の２番では関係代名詞の that が省略されていますが、どこかわかりますか。that を省略しないで、次のようにも表現できますね。

　　　The first thing that they noticed was that the window was wide open.

③ 名詞節を導く接続詞 that

　that の用法に関しては、これが一番むずかしいと思われます。Unit 3 で学習したように、名詞節は文中の主要素（主語、補語、目的語）となるほか、同格節になったり、前置詞の目的語となったりするからです。名詞節であると判断したら、それが文中でどのような働きをしているかを見きわめる必要があります。

　Ｑ１の４番の文では、that 以下の名詞節が動詞 noticed の目的語となっていますね。この目的節を導く that は省略されることが多く、３番の文では says の後ろの that が省略されていました。

　　　I want you to tell me where your father keeps that piece of paper that says (that) you own the land.

　Exercise の２番にある that は、補語となる名詞節を導いていますね。３番の最初の that も名詞節を導いていますが、この場合はすぐ前にある record を説明する同格節となっています。

④ 副詞節を導く接続詞 that

　この用法の that は、ほかの語句と相関的に用いられることが多く、目的・程度・結果などの意味を表します。Ｑ１の５番の文は、いわゆる so that ～ 構文で「～する

ために」と目的を表していますね。副詞節を導くthatは省略されることがときどきあり、5番の文を次のように表現してもよいのです。

Daisuke hurried to meet Miki at the elementary school so they could walk home together.

また、Exerciseの4番にある1つ目のthat節は、なぜI am sorryだと思うかを説明しているので、「原因」を表す副詞節です。

補足

thatは、It is[was] 〜 thatの強調構文に用いられることがあります。〜の部分が強調されている語句で、次の文ではDaisukeが強調されていますね。

It was Daisuke that found cigarette butts on the ground.

この文からIt, was, thatを取り除くと、もとの文（＝強調構文となる前の文）Daisuke found cigarette butts on the ground.となります。主語のDaisukeではなく、目的語（cigarette butts）あるいは副詞句（on the ground）を強調したければ、以下のようになります。

It was cigarette butts that Daisuke found on the ground.
It was on the ground that Daisuke found cigarette butts.

Unit 10

Let's Read a Mystery and Master Grammar

照応語句

Vocabulary 次の語句の意味を確かめ、音声のあとについて発音しなさい。 Track 19

kneel [níːl] 自動 ひざをつく

collapse [kəlǽps] 自動 くずれる、座り込む

veterinarian [vèt ərənéəriən] 名C 獣医

up to ～：〈よくないこと〉をたくらんで、企てて

mean [míːn] 形 卑劣な

keep an eye on ～：～を見守る、見張る

reconstruct [rìːkənstrʌ́kt] 他動 改築する、再建する

Listening イラストを見ながら *"The Samurai Treasure"* の続きを音声で聞き、次の質問に答えなさい。 Track 20

問1 犬のテツがぐったりとしているのはなぜですか？

問2 これからどうすることになりましたか？

問3 山田老人は、なぜ大輔たちの家の辺りにいたのでしょうか？

Reading 物語 *"The Samurai Treasure"* の続きを読み、下の設問に答えなさい。

Part 11 Tetsu Poisoned

The three children put on their warm coats and went outside, where they found Old Man Yamada kneeling over Tetsu. The dog was lying on the ground and not moving.

"Tetsu!" cried Hide. He ran to the dog and began petting his head.

"Big Takuma opened the window and dropped in a piece of poisoned meat," said Old Man Yamada. "I saw him do it. The dog ate it and then jumped (1)out the window to chase Big Takuma. He only got this far before he collapsed. I was trying to help the dog and didn't notice when Big Takuma went in through the window. He really went running out of there fast. What did you do to him?"

"Miki scared him," said Daisuke.

"Miki?" asked Old Man Yamada.

"Yes," said Miki. "And Big Takuma scared my spider."

"I see," said Old Man Yamada. "Let's get this dog in the car and take him to a veterinarian. We might still be able to save him."

He carried the dog and led them to his car which was parked down the road. The three children stopped before getting in. "What's wrong?" asked Old Man Yamada.

"I heard you kidnap children and keep them in your house," said Miki.

Old Man Yamada laughed. "(2)Is that what they say about me?" he asked. "You don't believe that, do you?"

"No," said Miki. "You're helping Tetsu, so you must be a nice man." She got in the back seat. Old Man Yamada laid Tetsu gently down on the seat next to Miki. She patted the dog's head and softly said, "Poor, Tetsu!" (3)The rest got into the car and they drove to the veterinarian's house. They woke him up. While he was examining Tetsu, they talked.

"Why have you been standing outside our house at night?" asked Daisuke.

"Did you see me?" asked Old Man Yamada. "I thought I was being secret. I don't like talking with people much. I keep to myself, but I watch what is happening in this town. I saw that the three Maeda sisters were taking an interest in you and your land."

"Why do they want our land?" asked Hide.

"I don't know," said Old Man Yamada. "But they want it pretty (4)bad. (5)They have been to the city hall asking about it, and they have hired a lot of men to look at it for some reason. They must think there is something there worth having."

"Samurai treasure?" asked Hide.

"Who knows?" said Old Man Yamada. "I just knew they were up to no good. I've known those three sisters since we were in kindergarten together. They have always been mean. They drove away all of their family — all except Big Takuma. And he's just as mean as they are. (6)When they started bothering you kids, I thought I'd keep an eye on you for a while."

"Thanks," said Daisuke.

"No problem," said Old Man Yamada. "Now tell me. Where is your father?"

"I don't know," said Daisuke.

The veterinarian came out and told them that Tetsu would be all right. "But he is sleeping now and needs to rest. He can go home with you tomorrow."

Exercise A **Choose the correct answer.**

1. Which of the following is correct?
    a. Big Takuma hit Tetsu so hard that he was dying.
    b. Tetsu ate the food Big Takuma gave him and collapsed.
    c. Tetsu noticed Big Takuma and chased him into the house.
    d. Big Takuma called Tetsu to come out of the window.

2. Who hesitated to get into Old Man Yamada's car?
    a. Miki.
    b. Hide.
    c. Daisuke.
    d. All of them.

3. Old Man Yamada knows
    a. why the Maedas want the land of the Kinoshitas.
    b. where the father of the three children has gone.
    c. what kind of people the Maeda sisters are.
    d. when and how the Maedas will get Kinoshita's land.

4. According to Old Man Yamada
    a. The Maeda sisters asked the city office about Kinoshita's land.
    b. They have been trying to get the samurai treasure.
    c. They know why Daisuke's father has gone away.
    d. They have hired a lot of men to reconstruct their house.

5. What will they do about Tetsu?
    a. The veterinarian will operate on him tomorrow morning.
    b. He will make him sleep for a few hours.
    c. Old Man Yamada will take care of him.
    d. The children will take him back home tomorrow.

Exercise B   Answer the following questions.

問1 　下線部(1)<u>out</u>および(4)<u>bad</u>の品詞と意味を指摘しなさい。

問2 　下線部(2)(5)(6)を日本語に訳しなさい。

問3 　下線部(3)<u>The rest</u>とは誰のことですか、日本語で答えなさい。

Grammar for Comprehension（問題）

同じことばを繰り返すのはくどい印象を与え、発展性にも欠けるため、別のことばで置き換えたり、簡潔に表現することが好まれます。こうした役目を果たす「照応語句」について学習します。まず、次の質問に答えてみましょう。

Questions

次の各文の下線部が指している内容を日本語で指摘できますか？

1. "I saw that the three Maeda sisters were taking an interest in you and your land."
   "Why do <u>they</u> want our land?"
   "I don't know, but they want <u>it</u> pretty bad."
2. "I heard you kidnap children and keep them in your house."
   "Is <u>that</u> what they say about me?"
3. Overhead a crow called out and was answered by <u>another</u> farther away.
4. He thinks I don't see, but I <u>do</u>.

Check Your Answers

クラスでQuestionsに対する答えを確認してから、Exerciseの練習問題に進みなさい。Questionsについての詳しい説明は、解説を参照しなさい。

Exercise 次の文中の下線部が指す内容を日本語で指摘しなさい。

1. Big Takuma opened the window and dropped in a piece of poisoned meat. I saw (1)him (2)do it. The dog ate (3)it and then jumped out the window to chase Big Takuma. (4)He only got this far before he collapsed.

2. Two cigarette butts lay there in the grass. Daisuke threw down the (5)one he had in his hand with disgust. (6)That made three altogether.

3. Papa made a ton of food and put (7)it in freezer bags in the freezer.

4. He owns more land than we (8)do.

5. Daisuke, come here and look out of the window. But (9)do it carefully.

6. "They say any kids who wander onto his property disappear and are never seen again."
"Oh, come on. You don't believe (10)that stuff, do you?"

Grammar for Comprehension（解説）

1 照応語句の役割を担う代名詞

英語で人称代名詞が多用される理由の1つは、名詞や名詞相当語句を短い1語で表現できるからです。その中でも、itとtheyはあらゆる物・ことを指すので、きわめて有用です。

Questionsの1番では、相手の発言にあったthe three Maeda sistersを指してtheyを用い、さらにその発言のour landを受けてitを用いています。人称代名詞を用いることによって、くどい印象がなくなるとともに、二人の発言のつながりを生むという効果も出ていますね。

指示代名詞のthis, that, these, thoseにも同様な役割があります。筆者（話者）に強めたい気持ちが働くと、itを用いるところにthatを使うことがあります。Questionsの2番では、you kidnap children and keep them in your houseという内容をthatで受けていますね。

thisは、今述べたばかりのことがら、すぐ次に述べようとしていることがらをひとまとめにして表現する際の語です。また、筆者（話者）が心理的に近いと感ずる意識が強く作用しているときにもthisを用います。もちろん、these, thoseは複数の

内容や概念を受けて（あるいは前もって意識して）用いられます。

2　そのほかの仕組み

まとまりのある英文を見てみると、以下のような方法もあることがわかります。

1）(the) other(s), another, one または such を用いて、同じ種類に属する別のもの、そのようなもの、という意味を表す場合：

　　Questionsの3番では、crowを繰り返してanother crowと言う代わりにanotherと表現し、「もう一羽の（別の）カラス」という意味を表していますね。

2）すでに述べられた人・物・ことを別の名詞で置き換え、限定する語をかぶせる方法：

　　Exerciseの6番では、人のうわさでany kids who wander onto his property disappear and are never seen againと言われている内容を指す名詞stuffを用い、下線部(10)のようにthatで限定して、that stuffと表現しています。

3）doを名詞や代名詞と組み合わせることによって、すでに述べられた動作を受ける方法：

　　Exerciseの1番の下線部(2)では、opened the window and dropped in a piece of poisoned meatと表現する代わりに、do itと言っています。5番の下線部(9)では、look out of the windowの代わりにdo itを用いていますね。

4）代動詞 do、代不定詞 to などを用いて動詞の繰り返しを避ける場合：

　　Questionsの4番に出てくるdoは代動詞で、すぐ前のseeの代わりに用いられています。したがって、I do = I see ということになり、「私は見てるの」という意味を表しているのです。

Unit 11

～ing の用法

Let's Read a Mystery and Master Grammar

Vocabulary 次の語句の意味を確かめ、音声のあとについて発音しなさい。 Track 21

figure [fígjə] 名C 人の姿、人影
reflect [riflékt] 自動 反射する
object [ábdʒikt] 名C 物、物体
construction [kənstrʌ́kʃən] 名U 建設（作業）
heave [híːv] 他動 〈ため息・うなり声など〉を吐く
sigh [sái] 名C ため息
troublemaker [trʌ́blmèikə] 名C トラブルメーカー、もめごとを起す人
get it：罰せられる、お仕置きする
trespass [tréspəs] 自動 不法侵入する

Listening 次ページのイラストを見ながら *"The Samurai Treasure"* の続きを音声で聞き、次の質問に答えなさい。 Track 22

問1　前田家の三姉妹はここで何をしているのですか？
問2　山田老人に向かって、どんなことを言っていますか？
問3　ここに琢磨も加わりますが、そこに現れたのは誰ですか？
問4　その結果、どうなりましたか？

89

Reading 物語 *"The Samurai Treasure"* の続きを読み、下の設問に答えなさい。

Part 12　Papa Returns

　　The sun was starting to come up as they drove home. When they got near the Kinoshita house, Old Man Yamada parked his car near the woods.

　　"Let's see what they were doing there last night," he said.

　　After they had walked into the woods, they began to find that many holes had been dug into the ground.

　　"What were they doing?" asked Daisuke.

　　"They must be looking for treasure," said Hide.

　　"Look," said Miki. She was pointing ahead of them. Three figures stepped out of the trees. The morning sun reflected off (1)<u>something that was on their heads</u>. In their hands they held (2)<u>long dark objects</u>.

　　"That's the samurai ghosts," gasped Hide. "They've come to protect the treasure. And they don't look happy to see us."

　　"Not quite," said Old Man Yamada. "You! What are you doing here? Get off these people's land!"

　　"It's Maeda land now," said one of the men. As the men walked toward them, the three children could see that they were construction workers wearing metal hard hats and carrying shovels. Hide (3)heaved a sigh of relief.

"We will see about (4)that," said Old Man Yamada. "Take me to (5)those three troublemakers."

The men took them to the clearing. There were many men there with heavy machinery. In the middle of it all stood the three Maeda sisters telling the men where to dig.

"What do you think you are doing?" shouted Old Man Yamada.

"We have a legal paper that says we have a right to dig here," said one of the sisters. "(6)The Kinoshitas have nothing that shows they are the legal owners of this land, so it goes to whoever claims it. Now YOU get off OUR land!"

Big Takuma laughed, threw down the cigarette he was smoking, and started walking toward them. Several big men followed him. "Now you're going to get it," he said. Old Man Yamada and the three children stepped back.

"Wait a minute!" Everyone turned toward the voice that had just spoken. (7)There, appearing through the morning sunshine at the top of the hill where the Kinoshita clan had made their last brave fight, stood a man.

"Papa!" cried Miki and she ran up the hill as fast as she could. Father hugged her close and began to walk down the hill. Behind him walked several policemen.

"I have here a piece of paper that shows we are the owners of this land," said Papa.

"Let me see it," said one of the sisters, reaching out her hand.

"You will see it at my lawyer's office tomorrow," said Papa. "Now get off of our land!"

One of the policemen spoke up. "You people are trespassing. You will all have to leave now."

"And you will pay for all the damage you did to these trees," said Papa.

Exercise A Choose the correct answer.

1. When did Old Man Yamada and the three children go into the woods?
    a. Early in the morning.
    b. Late in the morning.
    c. Early in the evening.
    d. Late in the evening.

2. What did they find?

    a. They found the samurai ghosts protecting the treasure.

    b. They found some construction workers walking toward them.

    c. They found many holes had been dug in front of the Kinoshita house.

    d. They found several people looking for treasure underneath the hot spring.

3. The three Maeda sisters

    a. wore metal hard hats on their heads.

    b. were working with shovels in their hands.

    c. insisted the land now belonged to them.

    d. drove away Old Man Yamada and the three children.

4. Which of the following is correct?

    a. Big Takuma attacked the three children with several big men.

    b. The Maeda sisters had bought the land from the city.

    c. Old Man Yamada fought with Big Takuma and was defeated.

    d. A lot of men were working in the woods with heavy machines.

5. Papa appeared

    a. with the legal document, which he showed to the Maeda sisters.

    b. with his lawyer accompanied by several policemen.

    c. at the top of the hill and declared the land was their property.

    d. from among the trees, ran to his children and hugged them.

Exercise B — Answer the following questions.

問1　下線部(1)と(2)は、それぞれ何だったのですか、日本語で答えなさい。

問2　秀典が下線部(3)heaved a sigh of reliefのようにした理由を日本語で述べなさい。

問3　下線部(4)thatが指している内容を日本語で答えなさい。

問4　下線部(5)those three troublemakersとは誰のことですか、日本語で答えなさい。

問5　下線部(6)(7)を日本語に訳しなさい。

Grammar for Comprehension（問題）

　〜ingも、英語を聞いたり読んだりすると必ずと言っていいほど出てきますね。このユニットでは、〜ingの用法に的を絞って学習します。まず、次の質問の答えを考えてみましょう。

? Questions

次の各文中の〜ingの用法を説明できますか？

1. Big Takuma started walking toward them.
2. What are you doing here?
3. They were construction workers wearing metal hard hats and carrying shovels.
4. There, appearing through the morning sunshine at the top of the hill, stood a man.
5. The three children went outside, where they found Old Man Yamada kneeling over Tetsu.

✓ Check Your Answers

　クラスでQuestionsに対する答えを確認してから、Exerciseの練習問題に進みなさい。Questionsについての詳しい説明は、解説を参照しなさい。

Exercise　次の各文中の〜ingの用法を説明しなさい。

1. He was interrupted by the sound of someone knocking loudly on the door.
2. "Thank you for coming to visit," Daisuke said, pushing his brother and sister and the dog back through the door.
3. Daisuke stopped and smiled at his two younger siblings playing in their secret place.
4. That night Daisuke was awakened by Hide pulling on his arm.

5. "Let me see it," said one of the sisters, <u>reaching</u> out her hand.
6. "Oh, Hide" said Miki, <u>squeezing</u> his hand tighter. "Someone is there!"
7. It looks like someone was <u>standing</u> behind this tree <u>watching</u> us.
8. The boys thought about <u>going</u> into the forest and <u>picking</u> berries for food.

Grammar for Comprehension（解説）

1　動名詞の用法

　〜ingは動名詞か現在分詞のいずれかです。動名詞は名詞相当語なので、「〜すること」の意味を表し、文の主語、補語、目的語または前置詞の目的語となります。
　Questionsの1番では、動名詞walkingがstartedの目的語となっていますね。Exerciseの2番にあるcomingや8番のgoing, pickingは、前置詞（forやabout）の目的語となっています。

2　現在分詞の基本的用法

1）**進行形**：常にbe動詞と共起するので、Questionsの2番にあったare doingのように、簡単に見分けることができますね。

2）**形容詞用法**：現在分詞が単独で名詞（または代名詞）を修飾する場合は名詞の直前に置き、〈+α〉が続いて形容詞句となっている場合には、名詞の直後から修飾します。Questionsの3番目の文では、wearing metal hard hatsも carrying shovelsも句を形成しているので、workersの後ろに置かれていますね。

3）**分詞構文**：*"The Samurai Treasure"*のような物語を読んでいると頻繁に出てくるのが分詞構文です。分詞構文は、接続詞を用いて結ばれた複文の従属節、または重文のどちらか一方の節の中にある動詞を〜ing化するとともに、その接続詞を省略して表現したものです。2つの節の主語が同一であれば、〜ing化するほうの主語を省略することになります。
　解釈する立場から見ると、〜ingの部分に込められた接続詞的意味内容を、そ

の文全体あるいは前後の文脈から決める必要があります。Questionsの４番目の文にある分詞構文のappearing through the morning sunshine at the top of the hillは、主語のa manが立っていた状態（＝付帯状況）を示していると考えるのが妥当な解釈でしょうね。

４）補語：Questionsの５番に出てくるkneelingのように、補語になる現在分詞は第五文型（SVOC）のC（＝目的格補語）がほとんどです。第二文型（SVC）のC（＝主格補語）として用いられる現在分詞は、keep ～ing（～し続ける）のような慣用表現に見られます。

補足１

Exerciseの１番では、knockingがすぐ前のsomeoneを修飾している現在分詞のように見えるかもしれませんが、前置詞ofの目的語の位置に使われている動名詞です。「誰かの音」(the sound of someone) というよりも、「ノックする音」(the sound of knocking) のほうが自然だからです。

この文全体の主語は、文頭にあるHeですね。この主語ではなく、ほかの誰か（＝someone）が「ドアをノックした」ことを表すために、knockingのすぐ前にsomeoneを入れたのです。このようなsomeoneのことを「意味上の主語」と呼んでいます。

動詞には必ずその動作を行う主体や、その状態を保有している主体があるはずです。動名詞などの準動詞にも必ず「意味上の主語」があるのですが、意味上の主語がSVのSと一致するときには自然に理解できるので省略されます。また、一般の人（we, they, youにあたる場合）が意味上の主語のときも、示すのを避けることが多いのです。

補足２

Questionsの５番の文に出てくるkneelingを、第五文型の補語ではなく、形容詞用法と見なすことはできるでしょうか？　構造上は、そうした理解も可能です。仮にそうだとすると、「ひざまずいている山田老人」を見つけたということになります。しかしながら、子どもたちが外に出てみると、そこに山田老人がいて、よく見てみると「テツのわきでひざまずいている」のがわかったと解釈するのが自然ですね。「ひざまずいている山田老人」だけを周囲の状況から切り取って見つけたとは考えにくいからです。

現在分詞がSVOCのCに用いられた第五文型の文は、このように、ある人（もの・動物）が、ある動作・姿勢をしている様子を全体として見たり、聞いたりするということを表現するために用いられるのです。

Column 3

"No, thank you." と言ったら……

　　大学1年生の太田和夫くんが、夏休みを利用してアメリカに短期留学しました。ホームステイしながらの留学なので、アメリカ人の家庭生活も体験できると期待に胸をふくらませて出かけました。暑い夏の日、やっとの思いでホームステイ先に到着し、決まりきった挨拶を交わすと、ホストマザーが "Would you like something cold to drink?" と勧めてくれました。喉が渇いていたのですが、はじめてお邪魔する家でもあり、遠慮がちに "No, thank you." と答えました。ホストマザーは "OK, then, I'll show you around the house." と言って、いろんな部屋に案内してくれました。結局、冷たい飲み物は出てきませんでした。

　　"No, thank you." を「いいえ、結構です」という日本語に置き換えて考えると、きっと相手は「そんなこと言わずに、ぜひ」と再度勧めてくれるであろうと期待することでしょう。ところが、"No, thank you." は相手の勧めを（固く）断るときに使う表現です。当然のことながら、ホストマザーは和夫くんの発言を英語本来の意味で解釈し、それ以上冷たい飲み物を勧めようとはしなかったのです。"Thank you. I'd like some coke." などと率直に伝えていれば、後悔することもなかったでしょう。こうして和夫くんは、いわゆる「カルチャーショック」を経験したのです。

　　言語と文化は密接に絡み合っています。英語を習い始めてごく初期の段階で、次のような挨拶の場面を学ぶことがあるでしょう。

　　Bill : Hello, Betty.
　　Betty : Oh, hi, Bill.

　　何でもないことのように思えるかもしれませんが、英米人はよく相手の名前を呼び合います。それも、親しい間柄ではnicknameを使って呼びかけます。William, Elizabeth, ThomasよりもBill, Betty, Tomのほうが言いやすいということもあって、nicknameを使う習慣ができたのです。話の途中で相手の名前を頻繁に呼ぶ習慣は、かなり徹底しています。そうした習慣がない日本人には、やりにくいことですね。

　　和夫くんは、留学先での大学生活やホームステイ先での家庭生活を送る中で、カルチャーショックを受けながら、英米文化を身をもって体験してきたことでしょう。機会があれば、あなたもぜひ海外に出かけて異文化体験をしてみてください。

Unit 12

Let's Read a Mystery and Master Grammar

総復習

Vocabulary 次の語句の意味を確かめ、音声のあとについて発音しなさい。 Track 23

proof [prúːf] 名U 証拠、証明
sneak [sníːk] 自動 ひそかに立ち去る、こっそり出る
charge [tʃάːdʒ] 他動 〈人〉に〈金額〉を請求する
soak [sóuk] 自動 浸る、つかる
descendant [diséndənt] 名C 子孫
benefit [bénəfit] 他動 〜に利益をもたらす、〜のためになる
neighboring [néibəriŋ] 形 近隣の

Listening 次ページのイラストを見ながら *"The Samurai Treasure"* の続きを音声で聞き、次の質問に答えなさい。 Track 24

問1 パパはどこへ何をしに行っていたというのでしょうか？
問2 前田の三姉妹が欲しがっていたという宝物は何だったのですか？
問3 その宝物は、その後どんな役に立ったのでしょうか？

Reading 物語 *"The Samurai Treasure"* の続きを読み、下の設問に答えなさい。

Part 13 The Samurai Treasure

That night Papa made dinner for his children and Old Man Yamada.

"I am sorry I had to leave you kids for a while," he said, "but I knew those people would not stop bothering us until I found proof that we owned the land."

"But why did you have to go so far away?" asked Daisuke.

"Well, I looked in the city office and there was no record of it," said Father. "(1)So I knew I would have to go to where they kept very old records. I saw that the Maedas had hired some very bad men to follow me and I didn't want them to come near you kids, so I had to sneak away. I'm sorry, but I had to go so quickly without explanation. I knew you could take care of yourselves for a few days. I had to go all the way to Kyoto. There after searching for a long time, I found the 200-year-old records. Our family didn't buy these woods, so there was no record of that, but (2)the family of the Daimyo that Samurai Daisuke fought for gave them to us as a gift. I had to go to their family records in Kyoto and get a copy to show the forest is ours. We shouldn't have any more trouble from the Maedas."

"But why did they want the forest so bad?" asked Hide.

"Because of the treasure in the ground," said Father.

"The samurai treasure?" asked Miki. "Underneath the hot spring?"

"No," laughed Father. "The hot spring is the treasure."

"What?" asked all three children and Old Man Yamada.

"There is a lot of hot water down there under the ground," said Father. "And (3)with it is a lot of natural gas. Enough gas to heat every home in this town. That's what the Maedas wanted. They wanted to get control of that gas and charge all the people in the town a lot of money to heat their homes and cook their dinners."

A lot of (4)new things happened in the next year. The three kids still had their forest to play in, but now there was a big pipe running through part of it that carried natural gas to all the homes in the town (even to the Maedas). The town thanked the Kinoshitas for giving them free heat and cooking gas, so they built a lovely outdoor pool that was filled up by the hot spring. Papa, Daisuke, Hide, Miki and even Old Man Yamada could soak in the hot water (5)any time they wanted to take a bath. And (6)the Kinoshitas all thanked Samurai Daisuke every time they used the bath, hoping that he was somewhere nearby watching and listening.

Exercise A — Choose the correct answer.

1. Papa couldn't find the legal document of their land in the city office because
    a. so many years have passed.
    b. the land was given as a gift.
    c. some bad men had stolen the document.
    d. forests are not officially recorded as property.

2. Which of the following is correct?
    a. Papa asked some people to take care of his children while he was away.
    b. Papa met several people who were descendants of the Daimyo.
    c. Papa had thought it might take him only a few days to get proof.
    d. Papa found the 200-year-old records on his way back from Kyoto.

3. Why did the Maedas want the forest?

    a. Because they were planning to construct a big hot spring resort.

    b. To get natural gas from under the ground and sell it.

    c. To help the people in the town heat their homes.

    d. Because they knew the hot spring would save them a lot of money.

4. The treasure benefited

    a. all the people in the town.

    b. only the Kinoshita family.

    c. all the homes in neighboring towns.

    d. not only people but also plants and animals.

5. The Kinoshita family

    a. no longer went into the forest.

    b. met the ghost of Samurai Daisuke and thanked him.

    c. built an outdoor pool and filled it with hot spring water.

    d. enjoyed what the treasure had brought to them.

Exercise B Answer the following questions.

問1　下線部(1)(2)(6)を日本語に訳しなさい。

問2　下線部(3)を普通の語順に書き直しなさい。

問3　下線部(4)の<u>new things</u>としてどんなことがありましたか、日本語で2つ指摘しなさい。

問4　下線部(5)<u>any time</u>の品詞と意味を日本語で答えなさい。

Grammar for Comprehension (問題)

　このセクションでは、英文を正確に読み取るための実践的な文法力を身につけることを目指して、さまざまな文法項目を取り上げて学習してきました。**"The Samurai Treasure"** に出てくる英文を素材にして学習したので、実際に **"The Samurai Treasure"** を読み進む際に役立ったはずです。

このUnit 12で **"The Samurai Treasure"** も結末を迎え、「英文解釈のための英文法」の学習も終了します。これまでに学習したことをもう一度整理しておきましょう。

? Questions

次の各文の下線部についての質問に答えなさい。

1. I am sorry I had to leave you kids for a while.
   問　whileの品詞と意味は？

2. I knew those people would not stop bothering us until I found proof that we owned the land.
   問1　botheringの用法は？
   問2　thatの用法は？

3. I had to go to their family records in Kyoto and get a copy to show the forest is ours.
   問1　andは何を結んでいますか？
   問2　to showは何句でしょうか？
   問3　the forest is oursは何節でしょうか？

✓ Check Your Answers

クラスでQuestionsに対する答えを確認してから、Exerciseの練習問題に進みなさい。Questionsについての詳しい説明は、解説を参照しなさい。

Exercise　次の各文の下線部についての質問に答えなさい。

1. They say (1)that before the Daimyo of the Kinoshitas fell, he gave Samurai Daisuke his treasure (2)and told him (3)to hide it (4)where the Maedas would never find (5)it.
   (1) thatの用法は？　　　　　(2) 何を結んでいますか？
   (3) 意味上の主語は？　　　　(4) whereの用法は？
   (5) 何を指していますか？

2. Daisuke got his brother and sister up (1)and off to school in the morning. At the end of the day, he hurried from his high school (2)to meet Miki at the elementary school (3)and Hide at the junior high so that (4)they could walk home together.

 (1) (3)何を結んでいますか？ (2)何句でしょうか？
 (4)誰（何）を指していますか？

3. I saw (1)that the Maedas had hired some very bad men (2)to follow me and I didn't want them (3)to come near you kids, so I had to sneak away.

 (1)thatの用法は？ (2)何句でしょうか？
 (3)意味上の主語は？

4. The three kids still had their forest (1)to play in, but now there was a big pipe (2)running through part of (3)it (4)that carried natural gas (5)to all the homes (6)in the town.

 (1) (5)(6)何句でしょうか？ (2)〜ingの用法は？
 (3)何を指していますか？ (4)thatの用法は？

5. The town thanked the Kinoshitas for (1)giving (2)them free heat (3)and cooking gas, so they built a lovely outdoor pool (4)that was filled up by the hot spring.

 (1)〜ingの用法は？ (2)誰（何）を指していますか？
 (3)何を結んでいますか？ (4)thatの用法は？

Grammar for Comprehension (解説)

1 語と語の関係

　英語には大きく分類して8つの品詞がありましたね。例えば、whileという単語の品詞は何でしょうか。「〜のあいだ」という意味の接続詞と答える人が多いでしょう。しかし、Questionsの1番の文に出てくるwhileは、forという前置詞の後ろにa whileと不定冠詞とともに用いられています。したがって、この場合のwhileは「（短い）

時間」という意味の名詞として用いられているのです。

　言語の学習において、固定観念は禁物です。Unit 1で見たように、品詞とは「文中における」単語の役割を整理・分類したものであることを忘れず、語と語の関係を見きわめるように心がけましょう。

　thatの用法、～ingの用法などについても、柔軟に対処する必要があります。前後関係をよく見て、それぞれの用法を確かめなくてはいけません。Questionsの2番の文にはbotheringとthatが出てきますが、その用法は何でしょうか。botheringはstopの後ろに置かれ、usが続いています。stopはwould notに続いていることから動詞のはずです。すると、このbotheringは動名詞でstopという他動詞の目的語になっていると断定できます。

　一方、thatの後ろを見るとwe owned the landと「主語＋述語＋目的語」を備えた語群が続いています。thatはこの語群を導き、直前にあるproofについて説明する役割を果たしているに違いない。したがって、このthatは（同格の）名詞節を導く接続詞であると確定できます。

2　文の構造と意味

　Unit 3で「語レベルでの関係が句レベル、節レベルでも成り立つ」ことを学びました。このことをQuestionsの3番目の文で確認してみましょう。

　この文は、I had toの後ろに続く原形のgoとgetを等位接続詞andが結ぶという構造になっています。前半部分では、goの後ろにto their family recordsという副詞句が続き、そのrecordsをin Kyotoという形容詞句が修飾していますね。後半部分では、getの後ろに目的語のa copyが置かれ、それをto showという形容詞句が修飾しています。showの後ろには接続詞thatが省略されており、the forest is oursはshowの目的語となる名詞節を形成していると判断できます。

　このように、語レベル、句レベル、節レベルいずれの場合でも、文の構造を見きわめながら、同時に文全体の意味を把握する作業を行ってはじめて、正確な英文解釈ができるのです。英文は意味ある内容を伝えるために表現されているので、常識的に判断すれば、書き手（話し手）の意図を理解できるはずです。

3　拡大と縮小

　伝えたい内容をどのように表現するのかは書き手（話し手）の判断によりますが、

1つの文があまり長くなり過ぎると、文の構造が複雑になり、読み手（聞き手）の誤解を生むことになりかねません。接続詞や関係詞は文を拡大するのに便利な手段ですが、SとVが何度も現れるという結果につながります。不定詞・動名詞・分詞という準動詞を用いるのは、文を縮小して簡潔に表現する工夫と言えるでしょう。また、照応語句も繰り返しを避けることによって、拡大することを防ぐ役割を果たしていると言えますね。

補足1

　　Unit 7の補足2で、関係副詞の先行詞が省略されることを指摘しました。その結果、関係副詞で導かれた語群は全体として名詞節になりますが、Exerciseの1番の文にある where the Maedas would never find it は、全体として副詞節となっています。これは、以下のように、省略された先行詞（the place）に加えて前置詞 at を補ってみると、その事情がわかるでしょう。

　　He told him to hide it (at the place) where the Maedas would never find it.

補足2

　　Unit 11の補足1で、準動詞の「意味上の主語」について解説しました。動名詞の場合は、「意味上の主語」を所有格にして動名詞の前に置くこともあります。現在分詞や過去分詞の場合は、そのままの形で分詞の前に置くのが普通です。
　　不定詞は、①for ～, of ～の形で不定詞の直前に置く場合と②不定詞のすぐ前に目的格の形で挿入する場合とがあります。Exercise 1番の to hide や3番の to come の場合は、②の方法ですね。
　　ただし、分詞の形容詞用法では、意味上の主語は現在分詞や過去分詞が修飾している名詞（代名詞）になります。また、不定詞の形容詞用法の場合も、被修飾語が意味上の主語となることがあります。

著者紹介

編著者 宮田　学（みやた・まなぶ）

名古屋市立大学名誉教授

名古屋大学教育学部卒業。オーストラリア国シドニー大学大学院英語科教育ディプロマ課程修了。著書に『リーディングとライティングの理論と実践』（共著、大修館書店）、『ここまで通じる日本人英語』（編著、大修館書店）、『誤文心理と文法指導』（共著、大修館書店）、『英語教育の理論と授業の構想』（単著、福村出版）、テキストに『英語で書いてみよう』（共著、三修社）、『保育英語の練習帳』（編著、萌文書林）など。

原作者 トーマス・バゥアリー（Thomas Bauerle）

名古屋市立大学語学講師

米国インディアナ大学卒業。同大学院にて文学修士号取得。著書に "Forty Stories of Japan"（共著、Fine Line Press）、小説に 'Love in the Time of Apocalypse'、'Held Down by Metal Bonds'（いずれも雑誌 "Ran Magazine" に掲載）、'The Umbrella Man'、'Toad Stranglers and the Eyeball Bridge'（いずれも雑誌 "Nagoya Writes" に掲載）など。

制 作 協 力

録音協力	英語教育協議会　録音事業部（ELEC）
録音	ジョシュ・ケラー（Josh Keller）
装丁	aica
イラスト	岡村奈穂美
DTP制作	坂本　芳子

サムライ・トレジャー
推理小説を読んで文法を征服しよう！

2014年12月22日　初版第1刷発行

編著者	宮田　学
原作者	トーマス・バゥアリー
発行者	服部　直人
発行所	㈱萌文書林
	〒113-0021　東京都文京区本駒込6-25-6
	TEL 03-3943-0576　FAX 03-3943-0567
	http://www.houbun.com
	info@houbun.com
印刷・製本	モリモト印刷株式会社　　　　　　　　〈検印省略〉

©2014　Manabu Miyata, Thomas Bauerle, Printed in Japan
ISBN 978-4-89347-207-6　C1082

落丁・乱丁本は弊社までお送りください。送料弊社負担でお取り替えいたします。
本書の内容を一部または全部を無断で複写・複製、転記・転載することは、法律で認められた場合を除き、著作者および出版社の権利の侵害となります。本書からの複写・複製、転記・転載をご希望の場合、あらかじめ弊社あてに許諾をお求めください。